DREAM CHASERS
KEYS TO OBTAINING GOD'S BEST FROM A BAD SITUATION

Copyright © 2017 Xavier Jones

Published by Godzchild Publications
a division of Godzchild, Inc.
22 Halleck St., Newark, NJ 07104
www.godzchildproductions.net

Printed in the United States of America 2017 - 1st Edition

All rights reserved. Except as permitted under the U.S. Copyright Act of 1976, this publication shall not be broadcast, rewritten, distributed, or transmitted, electronically or copied, in any form, or stored in a database or retrieval system, without prior written permission from the author.

      Library of Congress Cataloging-in-Publications Data
      Dream Chasers/Xavier Jones

      ISBN   978-1942705468 (pbk.)

      1.Jones, XavierS., Jr. 2. Inspirational 3. Purpose 4. Self-Help
      5. Ministry 6. Christianity 7. Spiritual 8. Religion

2017

TABLE OF Contents

Chapter 1.   I Am Joseph *[1]*

Chapter 2.   Is this God's Vision or My Vision? *[15]*

Chapter 3.   How Do I Manage My Vision? *[35]*

Chapter 4.   You Can't Afford Me *[53]*

Chapter 5.   My Gift Got Me Out *[71]*

Chapter 6.   I Need the Lord to Give it To Me *[93]*

Chapter 7.   Manasseh is Coming *[111]*

Chapter 8.   I Need to Reset *[135]*

Chapter 9.   It Didn't Kill Me *[153]*

I Am Joseph

*This is the account of Jacob's family line. Joseph, a young man of seventeen, was tending the flocks with his brothers, the sons of Bilhah and the sons of Zilpah, his father's wives, and he brought their father a bad report about them. Now Israel loved Joseph more than any of his other sons, because he had been born to him in his old age; and he made an ornate robe for him. When his brothers saw that their father loved him more than any of them, they hated him and could not speak a kind word to him. Joseph had a dream, and when he told it to his brothers, they hated him all the more. - **Genesis 37: 2-5***

Before you were born, God knew who you were to be. God knew your gifts. God knew your hang-ups. God knew your natural skills. God knew your proclivities. God knew who you would be in relationship with. God knew who you would have to cut off. God was never surprised by you. Nothing in your life happened by accident. God knew you. He called you. He assigned you to be…*a dreamer.*

God did not judge your future based on your past. God did not conclude about your destiny based on your current predicament. He has always known something about you that you have not always known about yourself; God knows, that locked up inside of all of that potential and purpose, is a dreamer and a giant slayer. He's always known that you have the power to dream your way out of anything. You have the creative prowess and the skillful ingenuity to make impossible things possible. You have the innate ability to raise dead things from the grave. You have the discipline and the insight to make worlds believe in what others before you deemed improbable. You are a walking-talking-living-breathing dreamer.

God knew who you were destined to be, before your parents thought you up. Before they fell in love, and before they had their first argument, God knew what his plans were for your life; and He divinely orchestrated everything in your life—even the difficult seasons—to properly align you for all that He has deposited inside of you. Like a check signed by the endorser to deposit the right amount of cash into the right account, God never lost count of your worth. He never misplaced you, or left you in the cold. He's been keeping you and sustaining you even when you are unaware of his presence. In the hospital room, when the doctors first held you for the first time, He selected certain nurses to midwife you into existence; because you are His unique design.

YOU ARE JOSEPH

Dreamers are his special children. You may not know it right now, but you are Joseph. You are a visionary. You are a dreamer. As a dreamer, God's vision has been released inside of you. As a dreamer, God trusts you to carry His ideas. As a dreamer, you will be hated by those with whom you are most familiar. As a dreamer, you will be judged by the very people you are called to liberate, and as dreamer, you might not be the popular person simply because of the purpose that is inside of you. You are a dreamer. And this book intends to help you to identify all of the necessary seasons, stages, and phases to help you to obtain God's best for your life…even when you are cultivated from a series of bad situations.

THIS HAPPENED TO DEFINE YOU

I can't tell you how many people I know, who have been diagnosed with a terminal disease—but they have confessed, at a later time, that they wouldn't have wished their diagnosis on anyone, but in retrospect, this pain produced and defined them as a person. I can't tell you how many children have grown up in difficult households, only to realize that God was using their ostracized marginalization as a means to help others to admit and confront their own brokenness. Have you ever experienced God turn something bad into something good? Have you ever heard the stories on television of the grieving mother who forgave the very person who fatally killed her child behind the wheel of a car while intoxicated? Certainly, all issues are independently specific to the person and the situation, but I want you to know that God often uses the raw materials of our regrets as a catalyst toward our future. As a Joseph, you have the insight like Joseph, the vision like Joseph, the optimism like Joseph, and the trials like Joseph. You have the perspective like Joseph, the pain like Joseph, but also the promotion like Joseph. You are Joseph. But you are not alone.

 I, too, am Joseph. I know my earthly name is Xavier, but my biblical name is Joseph. And as Joseph, I know what it's like to have a lot of people around me, but very few people for me. I know what it's like to be able to talk to everyone in the room and make them feel comfortable, all while feeling alone in that same room because I am isolated for being favored. I know what it's like to be misunderstood by my silence, and judged by my speech. I know what it's like for the Father to give you a gift that He doesn't give as freely and as frequently to others, and just because you are chosen to carry or wear that coat of distinction, your "brothers"—your siblings-or as David said, "the very ones with whom you took sweet counsel," despise the very ground you walk on.

No vision or dream comes to you without some level of distress, some level of disappointment, some level of frustration. I remember when my grandmother, one of my biggest supporters, passed away and it was time for me to minister her funeral. Prior to this, there were a number of family members that did not want me to do the funeral. For some reason they felt as if I was not called from God. They felt that I was too young and inadequate. They wondered how God raised up a young man to do this, at such a time as this. Often times when God wants to use you, family tends to be the greatest opposition. I remember walking in the doors of the church that morning, getting ready to deliver the message. The pastor of the church that we were using disrespected me and pretty much attempted to embarrass me in every possible way. But my understanding was that this

> *No vision or dream comes to you without some level of distress, some level of disappointment, some level of frustration.*

was a test and I had to pass this test, similar to Joseph's. I had to maintain integrity. The pastor started yelling out in such an ungodly manner that I had to wonder, *Was I really in a church?* But I later realized that there were other people watching and that they would later come back and tell me that they were thankful that I handled it with such integrity.

One thing about Joseph is that Joseph will never always be in the pit. You'll not always be where you started and God will find a way for those to come back to you and help you some way or another. To this day, some people have gotten saved, healed and delivered as a result of me maintaining my composure at that funeral. I had every excuse, every possibility, of responding back at the level that he responded to me. But I decided that God was going to get the glory. So I recommend to you today, that no matter what you're going through, no matter who the opposition is, that you will make up in your mind that, "I will maintain integrity, even in the midst of the process, in the midst of the pit, in the midst of uncomfortable situations. I will do what I need to do to maintain in this process."

NO MATTER WHAT...PRODUCE!

But I don't want you to get so distracted by your haters that you forget to produce. Joseph was a producer. He was productive, and he got the job done. In every season of his life, he carried God's favor and he produced. He produced results when interpretation was needed in prison. He produced results when commerce exchange and management of resources was required. He produced results by forgiving the very people who set him up, and wanted him dead—because Joseph knew how to turn the bad into good. Joseph didn't hold grudges. Joseph didn't do to others what they did to him, especially when they did him wrong. Like Jesus, Joseph learned the art of "blessing them that curse you," and "praying for them that despitefully use you and persecute you." Joseph learned how to take out the knife that was driven in his back, and still pray for the Judas in his camp.

If you are Joseph, you have a unique grace to lead. God has equipped you with wisdom and knowledge on how to deal with difficult situations. Your perspective is your greatest asset. To them, it is a pit. To you, it is a pre-requisite to a penthouse promotion. To them, it is a prison. To you, it is a dark room where God is developing his greatest asset. To them, it's a foreclosed house. To you, it's a non-profit home for single mothers and widow women. To them, it's just a piece of car. But to you, it is the instrument you drive to bring others to Christ. When you have a Joseph around, you can't help but to be pushed to your limitations, and beyond. Joseph is never going to allow you to be comfortable where you are, because he's destined to push you to where you belong.

Joseph is not just in the church. Joseph is all over the world. Joseph shifts government. Joseph shifts Hollywood and entertainment. Joseph sits on boards of hospitals, and encourages curriculum development in educational programs. Joseph is a dreamer, and a world-shifter. As I study the life and heart of Joseph, it is clearer to me now more than ever before that our failures have the power to teach us lessons that we would not have otherwise learned. In my opinion, failure is the first grade teacher that gives you permission to move on to the second grade. If it weren't for failure in one bad relationship, you wouldn't have learned to guard your heart in another. If it weren't for one bad failure of a financial investment, you wouldn't have learned to depend on attorneys and accountants to help guide your financial portfolio once you reached a 6-figure salary. Failure has a way of growing you up. Failure has a way of building you up. Joseph proves that. And if you are Joseph, you can't be afraid to fail. You can't be afraid to mess up. All throughout Joseph's life, he was placed in difficult situations. Some of those situations, he made the best decision with the information he had. Other times, he messed up (in the eyes of other humans). But with God, your failure isn't failure, because if you learn from it... it's tuition. If you learn from it, it isn't even a mistake—it was a necessary stepping-stone to get you to the palace where you belong.

> *If you are Joseph, then you need to accept that your life is a message and God is trying to produce something in you by producing something through you.*

If you are Joseph, then you need to accept that your life is a message and God is trying to produce something in you by producing something through you. What is he trying to communicate through you right now? What dream is God waiting to interpret through you for the world? How are you to take the principles of your life and amalgamate them with the purpose of your call, for God's glory and for your good? That is what I intend to walk you through in this book. It's important for you to take in all of the information that has been entrusted to me from God—downloaded directly from heaven. It is my prayer that as you unpack various episodes of Joseph's life in the Bible, that you will also be able to recognize the dream-chaser in your own.

QUESTIONS

1) How does your life compare to Joseph?

_____
_____
_____
_____
_____
_____
_____
_____
_____
_____
_____

2) What has God called you to produce? Who are you supposed to help?

_____

_____

_____

_____

_____

_____

_____

_____

_____

_____

_____

_____

_____

PRAYER

Below, Write a Prayer of Identity. Identify who you are and ask God to help you to produce.

_____

_____

_____

_____

_____

_____

_____

_____

_____

_____

_____

_____

_____

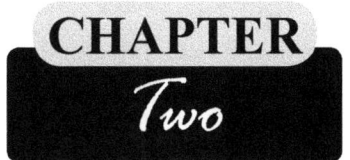

Is This God's Vision or My Vision?

*T*his worship project *The Sound*, Bishop William Murphy III wrote a song titled, "Dream" and I believe these lyrics will resonate with every dreamer who has ever had destiny locked inside of them.

It's never too late to be what you should've been
It's never too late to start over again
Dream

It's never too late to do what you should've done
The curses are gone you are the chosen one
Dream

It's never too late to chase after your dream
What God has prepared your eyes have never seen

Dream

Today is the day that God's gonna change your name
And after today you'll never be the same

Dream

Indeed, you are reading this book because you have a dream. God placed it in you before the foundation of the world, and over time, he will mature that dream and help you realize what he has called you to do. No matter how old you are, I agree with Bishop Murphy "It's never too late." God is a redeemer of time. God is a restorer of what you've lost. If God can impregnate Sarah and Abraham after they were past child bearing years, then surely God can resurrect your dream from the desiccating valley of dry bones and despair. I believe in the God of the impossible. There is nothing too hard for God, and He specializes in helping you to finish what you start. In that regard, it's never too late to chase. It's never to late to do. It's never to late to start. Why? It's because dreamers are given extensions to the deadline.

Have you ever been told by your teacher to submit a paper by midnight, but for whatever reason, you couldn't get the assignment done? Perhaps writer's block got in the way. Maybe you had a personal emergency. But you knew the rule: if you don't submit the assignment on time, you will not get credit. So you worked hard to finish the work, and at some point you realized: there's no way I can do excellent work under this much pressure. So you paused and wrote an email to the professor showing him the work you had done, and explaining the rationale behind your request for an extension. Oh what joy it was when you opened the response to their email with those heavenly words: your extension has been granted. A boost of new energy will hit your spirit when the teacher, who could've given you a failing grade, decides to overlook your tardiness, and bless you anyway?

Isn't that just like God? He knows that we sometimes procrastinate on the call. He knows that we do not always work with intensity and persistence on our purpose. But He grants us the favor of an extension—so that we are able to reap harvest from a ground that should've spoiled a long time ago.

GOD IS A GRACE DISPENSER

Dreamers, that is the grace of God personified. As beneficiaries of His grace, He gives us time to dream again and obey again. But make no mistake about it—eventually, your time will run out. Eventually, you will be asked to submit something to the Lord, and if you are not ready (after grace has been extended) then God just might give your dream to someone else. Consider this parable Jesus tells to His disciples in the gospel according to Matthew 25:14-29. The parable in Matthew 25 is a wake-up call for every dreamer. It is an alarm clock for the person who says "I can do this tomorrow." When you bury what God has given you, not only are you punished, but the talent that was supposed to bless you will be given to someone else. God might just give your blessing to someone else! He just might give your vision to someone else. This is not just a truth written in parables. This is proven all throughout scripture. When Saul did not obey God's command as King of Israel, God raised up David to do what Saul did not do. Worst of all, God allowed Saul to live and watch David reign as a better king in his place.

In your mind, which is worse—to not write the book God told you to write, or to walk into the bookstore and see your book with someone else's name on it? What's worse—to not step out on faith and launch the company God told you to launch, or to one day open up Forbes Magazine and see some CEO presenting your idea to the world, and making money from it—the same money that should've been in your pocket is now in someone else's. What's worse—to ask your secret crush out on a date, or to live frustrated as a single person for the rest of your life, as your friends enjoy the bliss of marriage because they had to courage to pursue their dream?

As dreamers, you must be thankful that God extends deadlines. You must appreciate the fact that God gives you the grace to build again, to dream again, and to start over. But at the same time, you must be passionate about getting the job done. Whatever you are to accomplish in the earth, and whatever God has downloaded into your spirit, do not allow the imp of procrastination to keep you bound one more second. Do what God said do, and do it now!

GOD'S VISION OR MY VISION?

The first essential step to help you chase God's dream and pursue God's purpose for your life is simple: *make a distinction between what God wants for your life, and what you want for your life.* The hardest thing to do, for many of us, is tell the truth about what we want versus what God wills. As you discern the dream God has deposited inside of you, ask God for clarity. Is this God's will or is this your wish? Is this the anointing leading you or ambition controlling you? In order for Joseph to walk into his God-ordained destiny, he had to line up with what God said about him. The will of God is

> *make a distinction between what God wants for your life, and what you want for your life.*

not a multiple choice test. There are not several careers you can choose, or several places you can launch your ministry, or several people you can marry—God is strategic and God is specific. If you want to reap the benefits of God's vision, you have to be clear about his vision. Quite simply, you've got to know the voice of God. Why? It's because there is a difference between your vision and God's vision. Your vision feeds your flesh. God's vision feeds the spirit. Your vision is about you only. God's vision is about the world. Your vision will create problems. God's vision will bring answers. Your vision is a human idea crafted from your mind. God's vision is a heavenly idea downloaded from your Creator. The same way you can't have your cake and eat it, too—the same is true with vision—you can't have your vision on the one hand and God's vision on the other; if you do, then what you create is DI-VISION.

DON'T TRY TO DREAM
IF YOU DON'T PLAN TO PRAY

Hear the words of Habakkuk 2 as guidance to avoid division. Scripture says, *"Then the Lord replied, 'write down the revelation and make it plain on tablets so that a herald may run with it."* There are several principles locked into this scripture that will help you to chase after God's dream for your life with clear perspective. First of all, the verse opens up with the words *then the Lord replied.* If the Lord replied, then there must've been a conversation happening between the Lord and Habakkuk before a reply was given. Habakkuk must've been speaking to the Lord prior to this verse because a reply presupposes that a request was made ahead of time. This leads me to our first Dreamer's Principle: *don't try to dream if you don't plan to pray.* A dreamer that doesn't pray isn't awake. They are sleeping until prayer happens. When we pray, our spiritual antenna is lifted and centered. When we pray, we are able to articulate our questions to God, in the hopes that he will respond. It's a dangerous thing to try to live without praying. It's a dangerous thing to try to lead without praying. When Joseph received a dream from God, he didn't leave it to his own thinking pattern. He went to his father and his brothers to get help. Many might argue that those were the wrong people to go to, but the point is, he went to the *father*. He went to a source greater than himself. When we receive heavenly ideas from God, we can't just rush to working, writing, and doing. We've got to pause and pray. When we pray, we not only become more sensitive to God, but we also remind ourselves that we are not our own God. God doesn't need our prayer to make Him aware of anything. God knows all about who we are and where we are. But prayer, for the believer, is for affirmation not information. When we pray, we affirm that we are not God and God is the only one who can interpret our dreams. When we are pray, we bow down to the idea that we know what we are doing, and we submit to the leading of the Holy Spirit. A visionary who doesn't pray is spiritually blind. He may know what to say. She may have a lot of skills. But their vision will not succeed until they bring their dream to God, and wait patiently for a reply.

WAIT FOR GOD TO SPEAK

The second dreamer's principle that Habakkuk 2 teaches us is to *wait for God to speak*. Habakkuk spends the first several verses of Chapter 1 venting off his frustration about the current predicament of his people. He feels discouraged, abandoned, and overwhelmed. But at the end of his venting session, he decided to wait by the tower and watch for the Lord to respond. This is powerful because many of us pray, but we get up and move as if God isn't going to respond. We pray out of habit or formality, but then we make our to-do list and move as if prayer was only a necessary pre-requisite that "pretends" to need God. Habakkuk doesn't so that. He determines to wait on the Lord, and not move until otherwise notified. In this day of microwaveable everything—food, love, and ministry—we may be tempted to move quicker than we need to. But if we learn to wait on God, we will save ourselves a lot of heartache and pain. When it's God's vision, you don't own it. You can't control it. So you have to wait on the Manufacturer to meet with you and speak to you about it.

GOD IS FAITHFUL TO RESPOND

The third and final principle that we glean from Habakkuk 2 in relationship to a God-sized-dream is this—*God is faithful to respond*. The Bible says, "and the Lord said to Habakkuk, 'Write'..." All throughout the Old Testament we see these words: and the Lord said the Jeremiah, and the Lord said to Adam, and the Lord said the Noah, and the Lord said to Hagar. If the Lord is faithful to say what needs to be said to everyone else, then surely he will speak to you. God is faithful to respond. Why? It's because it's God's vision. But most times, we are so caught up in our vision that we don't hear God speak. We also have a tendency to call ourselves, or speak on behalf of God and that isn't helpful either. And worst of all, we not only move before God speaks, but we speak FOR God. In other words, we construct an idea of what we think God is saying, long before He's actually said anything. Dreamers, listen to me: you will not succeed pretending to be God. You can't have your vision and ask God to sign His name on it. If you do, the check will bounce, and the bank in which it was deposited will reject your idea. God is the author and finisher of our faith. He is not the author and finisher of our fiction, or our fantasy, or our desires. His vision is clear—with or without your assistance. Our future is sure in Him because He is God. He is faithful when we are fickle. He is reliable when we are uncertain. When you are adamant about chasing the dream, you learn to put all of your trust in the one who gave it to you. You learn to write it down just the way He spoke it. God's visions are clear. They are always plain.

GOD SPEAKS IN YOUR LANGUAGE

God speaks in your language! God will never tell you a vision that He wants you to do that you don't understand. When He speaks, He will speak to you in a dialect that you comprehend, because He wants it to come to pass. It isn't as hard as we make it, but sometimes, we are operating on our vision and not God's vision. And when we do that, then our dreams will expire. Our hopes will fall, and our zeal will fail. But when we lean and depend on God, the way the 3 Hebrew Boys (Shadrach, Meshach, and Abednego) trusted in God who would deliver them from the fire, then we are able to watch, watch, and listen to the God who is faithful to speak when we need him the most.

> *God speaks in your language! God will never tell you a vision that He wants you to do that you don't understand.*

If you are struggling with DI-VISION in your life, you can't move on until you destroy the part of you that longs to be seen. You can't grow into all that God has designed you to be, if you haven't circumcised your heart in this area. Sometimes, we must die to what our parents told us we would become. Our parents are great advisors, but they are not God. Other times, we must die to what society deems as successful. It may sound good, but what did God say? How did God speak to you? What did you write down? Who were you before all of the bills, money, and fame got in the way?

I have learned that in accomplishing dreams, you have to realize that God doesn't play chess. God is the kind of God that plays Connect Four. He's the One who has the power to take stuff that happened to you from 2001 to 2008 and tie it all together for it all to make sense. I remember going to the Junior Orange Bowl Parade at the age of fourteen. For some reason I wanted to be a firefighter. I've attempted to get into so many other explore programs, which is a junior firefighter program, and I could never get in.

But while I was at this parade I had seen this group of people called Coral Gable's Fire Explorers. They were junior firefighters. I went up and I got information and later ended up attending the program. After being a part of the program, I went to college and came back and I was one of the first people out of that post to be hired as a real firefighter and paramedic. Who would have ever thought that going to a parade that day that God would have used that same place as a place that I would thrive in? That God would use the same place as me being one of the youngest firefighters and paramedics being hired and certified. Who would have ever thought?

Sometimes you have to go through and be intentional about listening to God, although it may be uncomfortable right now; it is God setting you up for what will happen next. As a result, God has given me the grace and given me the ability to operate in all facets of the department in one way or another. But it all started with my obedience in going to the Junior Orange Bowl Parade. I want to tell you today, listen to the still, small voice because maybe, just maybe, God wants to use you. Maybe it's time for a career change. Maybe it's time to go after that dream. Maybe it's time to go after that vision.

Just like He did for Abraham, I think he'll do it for you. He spoke to Abraham about stars because that was the level that Abraham was on. But then there are other seasons that He began to talk to Abraham in different ways. The way God starts to speak to you, doesn't mean that He's going to finish speaking to you that way. He started speaking to me about the Junior Orange Bowl Parade. But I believe He's going to finish speaking to me when I have the ability to rise through every rank of the department. Go after your dream. Go after your vision. Go after what God says.

Before you move on to the next chapter, revisit the dream. Write down the vision. Ask yourself, "is this from God or is this from me?" Once you have clarity about that, then you will be ready to give yourself away…so that God can use you.

QUESTIONS

1) What are you passionate about? What are you trained to do (vocationally, trade, educationally)?

_____
_____
_____
_____
_____
_____
_____
_____
_____
_____
_____
_____
_____
_____

2) How do you know this is God's dream for you?

3) Talk about a time when you were operating in your vision instead of God's dream. What did you learn?

PRAYER

Below, Write a Prayer of Clarity. Ask God to clarify the dream and separate it from your vision. Remember, God is the planner. We are the participant.

_____
_____
_____
_____
_____
_____
_____
_____
_____
_____
_____
_____
_____
_____

How Do I Manage My Vision?

For out of the abundance of the heart the mouth speaks. A good man out of the good treasure of his heart brings forth good things, and an evil man out of the evil treasure brings forth evil things" **Matthew 12:34-35**

Speak to my heart, Holy Spirit.

Give me the words that will bring you new life;

Words are the wings of the morning, the dark nights will fade away

...if you speak to my heart.

These powerful lyrics, sung by Pastor Donnie McClurkin are both a song and a prayer. They are words that every dreamer should pray daily. If it is true that good treasure comes from a good heart, then it is also true that a good vision comes from a good heart as well. So tell me *what's in your heart?*

In Chapter 2, we talked about the difference between God's vision and your vision. If you are being directed by God to carry out a vision, know this: *God's vision will first communicate to your heart and cause your heart to communicate with your head.* If your vision begins with your head alone, then you are thinking logically. But when God's vision in you begins in your heart, you are now thinking supernaturally. Everything God does (in us and through us) is simple. In short, God wants to help you see life through the lens of your heart. When you see with your heart, then like Adam, you will enjoy the Garden of Eden without seeing the tree of the knowledge of good and evil as restrictive. When you lead with your head, you see protection as restriction. But when you lead with your heart, you see life from a healthy place of possibilities, and not from a deficit.

Why is all of this important? It's because if you're going to do vision right, you've got to work on your sight first before you work on anything else. Think about what God says to Jeremiah when He trains him to be a prophet. He asks him in Jeremiah 1 *what do you see?* This is the first question God asks every prophet, every seer, and every dreamer; because if you aren't *seeing* right, then you can't *envision* right. If you can't answer what you see and identify the problem, then you will never get to a place where you can build a solution for that problem.

CHAPTER THREE

God's vision is 3-D. It has height, width, and depth to it. By that I mean, God gives you kaleidoscopic insight into His will for your life. When He gives you vision, He allows you to become a distribution center for His glory. He allows you to become the conduit by which His goals are produced. This is the heart of recognizing the difference between your vision and God's vision. Your vision will declare, "I want to be a millionaire." But God's vision will say, "I want to be a millionaire so I can finance churches that do not have the membership to fund their ideas. Your vision will say, "I want to have a big house and a big car for my own image. But God's vision will say, "I want to have money as a resource so I can become a helper to finance the gospel around the world."

> *The impact you will make in life will only be as great as your willingness to serve others.*

God's vision is never shallow. It's never about you. It always extends beyond you and it helps others to serve the world. Joseph's first dream proves it in Genesis:

> *5 Joseph had a dream, and when he told it to his brothers, they hated him all the more. 6 He said to them, "Listen to this dream I had: 7 We were binding sheaves of grain out in the field when suddenly my sheaf rose and stood upright, while your sheaves gathered around mine and bowed down*

to it." **8** *His brothers said to him, "Do you intend to reign over us? Will you actually rule us?" And they hated him all the more because of his dream and what he had said.*
Genesis 37:5-8

Joseph's brothers interpreted his dream with pride and selfishness. To them, this dream was about Joseph being above his brothers. They were intimidated by his assignment to lead the world out of a drought and an economic recession. But when you look at this dream through God's eyes, it was all about securing his brothers, not controlling his brothers. God raised up Joseph to make sure that his family would be sustained during the difficult seasons. Joseph wasn't above them; he was assigned to help them. God's vision is always about someone else. *The impact you will make in life will only be as great as your willingness to serve others.* When you think about your life, are you narcissistic or selfless? Do you plan your day around what you want to get accomplished, or do you make sure to think about others? When you pray, do you whisper a laundry list of things you want God to do for you, or do you intercede for our country, our world, and for our families? When you begin to live a life that is obsessed with God's vision, you will be able to change the world by changing your perspective.

I remember at the age of twelve, walking out of the house, down the street to a church and walking in that church and having no clue about God. But something in that service made me feel like I needed to give my heart to Jesus. I needed to change my life. Something more needed to happen. I went to that service and I gave my life to God. Subsequently, I got baptized. After I got baptized, I kept believing God that He would save my family. I could remember talking to them about God and they thought, "He's just playing games." I continued to go back and yet no one would move. I still reminisce on the days of my preteen years when I'd walk through the house and I'd pray. I'd touch every pillow and pray that God would save my family. I'd get in my sister's car and pray that God would save them. At that tender age I did not realize the effects of my prayers. If you're going to be a dreamer, you gotta have the ability to communicate with God. Why? It's because what God wants to do is raise up a generation and families that would do ministries together.

Many years later, God called me into the ministry as a pastor and I continued to pray and continued to believe God. My mother had gone through a series of sickness, series of pain and still she would say, "I'm not going to God. I don't want to play with God. I want to be perfect when I go to God."

But I later found out that what God was doing was to show me that all things are possible. It's like it was yesterday; May 1st, 2012, she walked into the church and she gave her life to God. As a result, my sisters, my brothers, all of my family gave their lives to God. The prayers that I had been tirelessly praying for years, the times that I laid in bed and prayed, the times I walked in their room and prayed; now it all made sense.

God has the power to bring all things together and cause it to work for His good and His glory. I want you to understand, that as a believer, that God is calling you to believe Him for the impossible. He's calling you to do that. But the faith that I used to believe for my mother and my father is the faith that I use for the whole city of Miami to come to God. It is the faith that I use when it's time for me to respond to an emergency call. But what I thought was developing me in only one area; it was developing me in every area. I like to tell people when you deal with God, you pray for one thing but He gives you what you're praying for and gives you some extra stuff added on to it. So in other words, you're getting two for the price of one. Walk in God's dream, walk in God's plan, walk in God's purpose, because maybe, just maybe, it's working out a greater cause and a greater victory.

RULES FOR MANAGING VISION

After your perspective has been purged, and after you can clearly see every dream through the lens of helping others, then you must learn how to manage the vision God has entrusted to you. When someone passes away, the deceased individually will usually leave a written will to bequeath their possessions and their investments into trustworthy hands. In the same way, when God puts vision in your heart, He has willed it to you for a reason. You can squander that vision the same way inheritors squander their inheritance, or you can manage it properly. In biblical terms, we call this stewardship. Here are the practical principles that will help you to manage the vision God has given to you.

Rule #1: Be careful with whom you share your dreams. Joseph told his dreams to his brothers and they hated him all the more. They were intimidated by his insight. They were annoyed by his very presence. Joseph wasn't the oldest, and he most certainly wasn't the best brother in his sibling's eyes, but he was the one whom the father favored. Joseph didn't ask for his dream. He didn't vote for his prophetic wisdom. He was given something he didn't know would change his life, without his permission; and still he was hated.

But what Joseph teaches us about distributing and

disseminating our vision is this: everybody will not celebrate you! You know why? It's because vision makes you different. Vision makes you peculiar. Having a vision will make you stand out—especially if others around you don't see what you see, and have the favor that you have. As you manage vision, you must learn to discern the right person to share your dreams with. Everybody in your corner does not have your back. Everyone in your church is not celebrating your promotion. Everyone who has your last name does not always want to see you make it. Wisdom says not only to guard your heart, but to guard your dreams.

GUARD YOUR HEART AND GUARD YOUR DREAMS

You must guard your dreams because God is moving you from where you are to where you are going. As a result, you are slated to be different. You are destined to be a paradigm shifter. That's the reality of your life. Some people can handle your valley, but they can't handle your mountain. Some people can take you when you're small, but they don't know what to do with you when God begins to expand you. This is why, very often, when God changes your level, He will also change your circle. When God brings you into fame, He will also bring you new friends.

Gone are the days when you have to downgrade your anointing just to accommodate someone else's insecurity. Gone are the days when you have to walk on eggshells just to be who you are. God is bringing you into a season of perpetual blessings and unapologetic access. You must be willing to manage your vision responsibly, and that always begins with who you share your dreams with. I had to learn the hard way. As a young pastor, I have seen the spirit of competition infiltrate the church in so many dangerous ways. I've seen people celebrate what God is doing with my church, and I've seen people try to duplicate what God is doing with my church. Clones are never called. Clones never get anywhere. I've had to take my stretching season with stride and confidence. I've had to close some doors, and allow God to introduce me to others who are genuinely happy for me. I had to learn not to apologize for my better and I had to be OK with divine eliminations.

DIVINE ELIMINATIONS

A divine elimination is orchestrated by God to bring you higher. When these occur, God will often hurt your feelings to protect your faith. But it will worth it in the end. Just like Joseph, when you share your dream with people who don't mean you any good, the first thing you will experience is rejection. This will cause you to then question whether God spoke to you or not. Certainly, in our minds, God speaks and the people support. But sometimes, the very people you take counsel with are the very people who will challenge your anointing. Jesus was brought into the world to heal the very people who put Him on a cross and crucified Him.

Sometimes rejection, not acceptance, is confirmation of God's vision.

Sometimes rejection, not acceptance, is confirmation of God's vision. After you experience the season of rejection, then you will receive a new level of protection and direction. Rejection helps you to turn around. Rejection helps you to come to yourself, separate your co-dependent behavior from the props you used to need to thrive, and it teaches you to rely solely on the voice and vision of God. Rejection also protects you from casting your pearl to swine. It helps to keep you focused on the people for whom you are called, instead of begging folks to accept you when they are not mature enough to even handle you.

Rejection and elimination altogether teach you who can handle your greatness at maximum speed. You've got to be ok with going alone sometimes. You've got to be able to swallow this hard pill: some people can't be with you because they don't share the same vision as you. And this is why God eliminated them from the running's. If He did not eliminate them, you wouldn't have gotten to the place where you are. During the season of elimination God strengthens your weaknesses. He guides and steers your ship. Do yourself a favor: don't try to put into people what God left out. If they don't have it, dragging them along won't fix it. Had Joseph not distanced himself from his brothers, he would've compromised his call. If Joseph did not experience God shifting his life through rejection and pain, he may not have become all that he was destined to be. *Sometimes God allows you to endure pain temporarily so that he can bring you joy for a lifetime.* Sometimes, even

> *Sometimes God allows you to endure pain temporarily so that he can bring you joy for a lifetime.*

if it's for a season, God will separate you from those you love—even your family—so that you can truly get a bigger picture of the vision he has invested in you.

THE WHO MATTERS SOME BUT THE WHEN MATTERS MORE

After you figure out who you need to share your vision with, you then need to figure out when to share your vision. Timing matters. Have you ever called someone and needed to vent to them about something serious, but they were on their way to a meeting? Have you ever had someone cancel on you when you pulled up at the restaurant where you had scheduled your meeting? Timing matters. It's not always what you say to whom, it's also important to think about when you say it as well.

Not everyone is on the same level as you right now. Every visionary will experience different seasons of their vision. If one visionary is in a dry season, you telling them about your vision will only cause them to feel jealous toward you. If some of your friends are struggling with their finances, you telling them about your promotion at work may feel like salt on their wound. The who matters and the when matters.

If you don't guard these two areas, people will try to talk you out of everything God has ordained you to be.

QUESTIONS

1) On a scale from 1-10, how good of a manager are you? Are you punctual, efficient, administratively graced, organized, and able to communicate your vision to others?

_____

_____

_____

_____

_____

_____

_____

_____

_____

2) Who do you trust to share your dream with? How do you know they are trustworthy?

_____

_____

_____

_____

_____

_____

_____

_____

_____

_____

_____

_____

_____

_____

3) Name a time when you shared something prematurely, and it did not help you to move the vision forward.

PRAYER

Below, Write a Prayer of Clarity. Ask God to clarify the drBelow, write a prayer for better management. Identify the areas of strength and weakness in your life, and ask God to help you to manage his vision better.

_____

_____

_____

_____

_____

_____

_____

_____

_____

_____

_____

_____

CHAPTER Four

You Can't Afford Me

It came about after these events that his master's wife looked with desire at Joseph, and she said, "Lie with me." But he refused and said to his master's wife," Behold, with me here, my master does not concern himself with anything in the house, and he has put all that he owns in my charge."There is no one greater in this house than I, and he has withheld nothing from me except you, because you are his wife. How then could I do this great evil and sin against God? **Genesis 39:7-9**

Have you ever gone shopping with someone who loves to look but not buy? I don't know about you, but it is one of the most annoying things in the world, to go to the mall with a group of people who try on clothes, ask for different shoe sizes, parade around in the fitting room…only to put the clothes back on the rack and walk away. People like this want to enjoy the idea of luxury, but the truth is, they can't afford what they are shopping for. Usually, those who can afford it, don't take long to buy it. With one look, they see what they want, they give the cashier their credit card, and they walk out with the item. The same is true in life. Some people are close to you because they are impressed by what they see. You may think they are here to stay, but the truth is, they are window shopping. You may think they want to invest their lives into you, but the truth is they are in love with the idea of being around something valuable, because they lack value themselves. What do you do when favor makes you unaffordable? What do you do when you feel like the odd ball? How do you manage the lonely seasons when you are over-qualified, or make too much money, or have too many things going for you…and everyone assumes that someone else has your heart, but the truth is, you're all alone? If you have favor like Joseph, you will have to accept that some people want to be around you, but the truth is, they can't afford you.

In Genesis 39, we are introduced to a woman whose name is never given. We are told who she is based on who she is married to. This woman is Potiphar's wife, which tells us that she already belonged to someone in marriage, and still, she is out shopping for another man. When lust is leading you, you will always shop in the mall for something you already have at home. Potiphar's wife is attracted to Joseph. He is a strong man. He is a handsome man. But I want to suggest that she is attracted to something else. She, my friends, is attracted to his favor. His favor has several components that are attractive to the eye, but too expensive for purchase.

THE FOUR ASPECTS OF FAVOR

When you are favored, you must recognize that favor is fuel for your dream. The dream can't come to pass unless favor creates opportunities for you to get from the pit of your betrayal to the palace of your blessing. Favor is fuel, and everyone loves fuel. Everyone loves when you can charge them, excite them, and ignite them. When you have favor, you have fresh ideas. When you have favor, you can turn any situation into a good situation. When you have favor, people will wait for days to have a conversation with you because they know that you have the ability to fuel their future into limitless possibilities.

For every favorable person with fuel, there is also the pain of isolation. Notice that Joseph had favor in the house with his brothers. He had favor in the pit. He had favor in the prison, and he had favor at Potiphar's house, but Joseph was also alone. In every season of his life, you only saw Joseph and his favor. You didn't see Joseph with another woman until later on in the story, and right now, in Potiphar's house

I can imagine that Joseph is isolated. Have you ever been isolated with favor? The world thinks you are so excited about life because everything comes to you without much effort, but the truth is, you're home trying to figure out why nobody loves you. It's amazing how you can be fuel to so many, and be running on empty yourself. When you have favor as fuel, you have to be careful to protect your seasons of isolation. Don't neglect prayer and devotional time with God because the only way to stand against the wiles of the enemy is to use your weapons of mass destruction. We don't wrestle with flesh and blood. We wrestle against principalities and rulers of darkness in high places. Potiphar's wife wasn't the enemy. She was used by the enemy of darkness to try to distract Joseph from his destined place, but thankfully Joseph realized, "she can't afford me."

When you are favored, you are also valuable. You receive connections in ways that others don't. Consider the text again. Joseph is now the second in command in Potiphar's house. He has complete jurisdiction and decision-making power over everything in the house, except Potiphar's wife.

But let's imagine how this wife must feel, seeing this new guy taking all of her power. If you were someone's wife, and you saw another young man come in to your palace and get access to all of the secret rooms, you might have a problem with that. But Joseph was valuable—and in some cases, Joseph may have been more valuable than Potiphar's wife, and no woman wants to be second to another man! Potiphar's wife didn't even realize that, laced inside of her attraction to Joseph, was her antipathy for Joseph. There's a thin line between love and hate, and sometimes your haters hate on you because deep down, they love you. They love your value. They love when you're around. They hate when you show up, but they look for you when you arrive.

Could it be that Potiphar envied the value on Joseph's life and that is why she wanted him all the more? She knew she couldn't afford him with the money in her account, but she also knew if she could get him to fall, then everything he owned would belong to her. When you know your value, you must protect your value. Stop giving do-overs to people who treat you like leftovers. Stop telling Delilah where your strength is, Samson! Don't allow people to manipulate you out of your favored place. It is so important in this season that you love yourself enough to say no to distraction. Love yourself enough to walk away from anything that depreciates your value. Love yourself enough to run in the opposite direction when you see seducing spirits enter into your personal space. Because you are valuable, you are connected to resources. Joseph had access to money he didn't earn, all because of his favor. When are you going to see that some people don't want you for you; they want you for who you know, and what you are connected to?

Thirdly, favored people understand that favor is a divine usher. Favor will escort you into doors you did not see coming. Favor will help you to prepare for opportunities you didn't know were happening. Favor is an usher, and favor is a motivator. It will help you to run away from things that are trying to assassinate your destiny. When Potiphar's wife attempted to corrupt Joseph, the Bible says he ran away. In his own strength, he may have fallen into the trap. But with God's strength, favor gives you the power to run away.

What are you willing to run away from to make sure that the will of God is accomplished in your life? Joseph ran from Potiphar's wife. What are you willing to run from? Are you willing to run away from the temptation to date "potential" when God wants you to marry "purpose"? Are you willing to run away from a job that makes you feel uncomfortable and boxed in? Are you able to run away from more money if it means you will be more miserable? The level of your favor is determined by your willingness to run. Scripture says resist the devil, submit to God and he will flee. Flee fornication. Why? Because the enemy knows if he can convince you to walk and not run, he will be able to catch up to you and destroy your purpose. But Joseph ran. Sometimes you have to run away from trying to get in God's way. You know, Sarah and Abraham didn't wait for God, and they decided to help God to accomplish his will. In doing so, they created Ishmael, they hurt Hagar, and a larger problem ensued because of their inability to run away from impulsivity. In this season, you've got to learn how to run from it all. Run from the fear that says God has forgotten about you. Run from the tears of yesterday's pain. Run until you see the promise in clear view. The only person stopping you from getting to the promise, is YOU!

Fourthly, favored people must manage their life with integrity. When I look at the story of Joseph, I see a man who had integrity even after he was falsely accused. I'll never forget a situation that happened to me about seven or eight years ago. I had just finished college, and at the time, I was thriving in ministry and God began to open up amazing doors for me. That is, until rumors were spread about me that called into question my identity. To add insult to injury, these rumors were uttered by close friends. They decided to get together one day and conspire a plan to destroy me. They went to my pastor and he believed everything they said. He didn't vet the situation or investigate. He took their word for truth, and soon after, he asked me to sit down for a while. He told me that I could no longer be a minister, and never took the time to verify if the stories/rumors/lies were true. But when you have integrity, you recognize that vengeance belongs to the Lord. You don't fight because the battle isn't yours to fight. It belongs to the Lord. It was hard to go in that church and see what, at that time, felt like the destruction of my ministry. But God had a plan. The same way that Joseph went to prison for something he didn't do, God used that situation to build character in me. I was humiliated, but God got the glory in the end. Joseph never did anything wrong, but Potiphar had him imprisoned because of his integrity. Do you have the integrity to go to prison even if you didn't do anything wrong? Do you have the power to stay silent when others are falsely accusing you and speaking all manner of evil against you? That season of my life taught me that I can't trust people, even if I call them my friends. I can only trust God. That season in my life taught me how to invest in ministry so that I didn't develop hidden animosity. Now I know that when I serve the church, I am serving the Lord. If the people disappoint me, it's all good because I am serving the Lord who reigns above it all. Those "friends" thought that their distraction would destroy me. They thought that my young age would eliminate me from future opportunities. But what God has for you, is for you, and nothing better prepared me for my current season, than my past pain.

My friends were mad because they couldn't afford me. There was a grace on my life that made them upset, and the same can be said about the favor on your life. If Potiphar isn't upset, you're doing something wrong. If his wife isn't accusing you of drama, you're doing something wrong. When you have the power to have integrity in the midst of calamity, that's confirmation that you're favored.

HOW TO MANAGE THIS SEASON

So practically speaking, how do you manage being favored, valued, hated on, and falsely accused? What lessons can we glean from my testimony and Joseph's story to help you to keep moving in the direction of destiny? First, you must learn the gift of separation. Joseph learned how to remove himself from toxic situations. That means you need to silence every voice, turn up the voice of God and allow the Holy Spirit to minister to you. You will be in pain for a short time, but weeping may endure for a night. Joy is promised to come in the morning. If you want to move forward in this next season, embrace separation as a blessing and not a curse. The very friends you are breaking your back to keep, are the enemies that were stabbing you in your back, hoping you would die. Don't retaliate. Bless them that curse you. Pray for them that despitefully use you and persecute you. Be the bigger person. Decline phone calls from gossipers. Surround yourself with likeminded thinkers. Know your value enough to say no to some invitations.

Secondly, you must know your enemy. The enemy is our ex. He knows exactly what we like. He knows when we like it. He knows how we like it. The enemy studies us. In order for you to conquer in this next season, you're going to have to study him. You have to study your opponent. You can't let your weakness keep you weak. You're going to have to study the defensive line-up. Study the seasons when he introduces himself in your life. Study the vulnerable moments. Study and discern. Discern and study. *Be strong enough to admit when you're weak, and be weak enough to ask the Holy Spirit for strength.* Remember, we can choose the sin but we can't choose the consequence. As a single man, I know my weakness. I have studied my enemy. So when I received a wonderful promotion as a firefighter on my job, and when people come to my church to hear me preach as a pastor, I know that everyone is not walking into those doors with a pure motive. I've had many women walk up to me and say that God told them I was their husband. But I quickly respond, "God never told me that!" and I walk away. You've got to learn how to walk away. Don't entertain the enemy. Resist at all costs, and study your opponent so that the enemy doesn't catch you by surprise.

> *Be strong enough to admit when you're weak, and be weak enough to ask the Holy Spirit for strength.*

Thirdly, you must find accountability. You can't do this alone. Maybe Joseph going to prison was not punishment. Maybe God was introducing him to people who would be with him in painful situations. The baker and the butler were two people who came into Joseph's life during a painful season. The baker forgot about Joseph in the beginning, but in the end, the baker was a key person responsible for getting Joseph out of prison. Sometimes, God will introduce you to people in your prison who will help you to manage your pain. You've got to find accountability partners to help you through this season. In the multitude of counsel, there is safety. You need people who love you enough to tell you the truth. You need people who will cry when you cry, and who will look at you and tell you when you've cried enough. If you don't have counsel, then you are making every decision without checks and balances.

Fourthly, obey God no matter what. It's true what the Bible says: obedience is better than sacrifice. Joseph obeyed God in every season of his life, and God rewarded him greatly. I can remember in 2009, an opportunity presented itself for a special project at work. No one wanted it, but I was determined to learn and take on a new challenge. I prayed about it and I went to assist the person who was about to retire. It was very challenging, but it gave me so much insight that I didn't know I would need in the future. It was a lot of work, but it opened the door for me to sit at the table with key decision-makers. That one decision gave me the opportunity to meet the city manager, and now community leaders know my name. In many cases, people who make decisions, are calling me for my opinion. I'm telling you:

one decision to obey, opened up a reservoir of opportunities. I wonder what's on the other side of your obedience. I wonder what God can do through you if you refuse to settle for people who can't afford you.

QUESTIONS

1) Name a time when you settled in life—whether for love, or for a job, or for a relationship. Why did you settle? What did you learn?

___

___

___

___

___

___

___

___

2) How do you know you're favored. Re-read the four aspects of favor and identify the traits that pertain to you.

3) What are you willing to run away from to make sure that the will of God is accomplished in your life?

PRAYER

Below write a prayer of commitment. Commit to be all that God wants you to be and refuse to settle for anything less than God's best.

_____

_____

_____

_____

_____

_____

_____

_____

_____

_____

_____

_____

_____

My Gift Got Me Out

Then the chief butler spoke to Pharaoh, saying: "I remember my faults this day. When Pharaoh was angry with his servants, and put me in custody in the house of the captain of the guard, both me and the chief baker, we each had a dream in one night, he and I. Each of us dreamed according to the interpretation of his own dream. Now there was a young Hebrew man with us there, a servant of the captain of the guard. And we told him, and he interpreted our dreams for us; to each man he interpreted according to his own dream. And it came to pass, just as he interpreted for us, so it happened. He restored me to my office, and he hanged him."

Then Pharaoh sent and called Joseph, and they brought him quickly out of the dungeon; and he shaved, changed his clothing, and came to Pharaoh. And Pharaoh said to Joseph, "I have had a dream, and there is no one who can interpret it. But I have heard it said of you that you can understand a dream, to interpret it." **Genesis 41: 9-15**

Back in the day, when you walked into someone's home, you typically saw (upon first entering the house) a living room, a dining room, and a common living area. Houses are decorated differently now and furniture pieces are consistent with the owner's personality, but generally speaking, the classic dining room set had two distinct pieces of furniture. First, there was a long beautiful table with décor and fancy plate settings atop the table. As well, there was a china cabinet on the wall with great lighting and pristine glass windows in the dining area. Inside of that cabinet were other ornate china pieces, expensive plates, glasses, and utensils. Most would keep these expensive pieces in the cabinet all year long, and would only pull them out on special occasions. Nothing was wrong with the china; they were just set apart for special occasions. The value of the product was proven by the delicate manner in which it was handled. In my home, we used these pieces on Thanksgiving, Christmas, and whenever the pastor came over to eat. These pieces were too valuable to use for daily, mundane purposes. This is what it means to be set apart.

SANCTIFIED AND SET APART

Every dreamer has been set apart by God for a purpose. To be set apart means to be separated from. It means you have been distinguished by and differentiated apart from others. The thing that makes you different is also the thing that gives you value. So understand this: some people will want to remove themselves from your life by no fault of your own. They don't appreciate the fact that your difference brings you value, and as a result, they will hate you because you've been set apart by God for a purpose. Some people don't like that your value is confirmed by the way others handle you, honor you, and the way others appreciate you. But this is God's favor on your life. This is your coat, Joseph. This is your child, Mary. This is your vision, Habakkuk. This is your assignment, Jeremiah. God has uniquely designed you for special purposes—and you've been placed on reserve not for your punishment but for your preservation.

This idea of "being set apart because of your gift" is glaringly apparent in the life of Joseph. Before he turned 18 years old, his brothers wanted to destroy him as a young lad. They conspired to throw him in a cistern, hoping that he would die. But the cistern into which Joseph was thrown, was empty and without water. God preserved Joseph's life even when his brothers wanted to throw him away. Why? Because God preserves and protects those whom He sets apart.

and they took him and threw him into the cistern. The cistern was empty; there was no water in it. ***Genesis 37:24***

There are two reasons to praise God today! First, God kept you after you were overtaken. But second, God protected you from things that tried to overtake you. In this scene, Joseph was protected from what could've destroyed him and killed him if the enemy had had his way. Dreamer, one sign of your favor is not just in the things you can see… it's also in the empty cisterns you can't see. You could've drowned before you reached your destined place, but God kept you, preserved you and allowed you to rise above the insults, rise above the negativity, rise above the hatred, and rise above the betrayal. This is another sign that you were sent by God. If you ever doubted your anointing, just recall all of the things God has protected you from. Through dangers seen and unseen, through battles lost and won, through terrible situations and "almost" circumstances, God did not let you fail. He did not let you fall. If you found yourself slipping, look at it this way: now you know what to avoid. Now you know who to invest in. Now you have experience. Now you have tips for the journey, and that will serve as wisdom for your posterity. If you learned from it…

> *Don't neglect prayer and devotional time with God… We don't wrestle with flesh and blood.*

it's not a mistake…it's tuition!

David was also a dreamer who was hated by his siblings. The moment it became clear that David was unique and that the oil of God would flow on David's head, his brothers developed great antipathy toward him.

> *When Eliab, David's oldest brother, heard him speaking with the men, he burned with anger at him and asked, "Why have you come down here? And with whom did you leave those few sheep in the wilderness? I know how conceited you are and how wicked your heart is; you came down only to watch the battle."* - **1 Samuel 17:28**

Think it not strange when those who are close to you begin to hate on you. Think it not strange when those you live with, want you to leave them alone. Think it not strange when those you enjoy being around, no longer want to be around you. These are the side-effects of favor. Some favor feels good because it opens doors you could not open for yourself. But most favor feels unfavorable because only a few people can handle you at your best. Most people would love to see you wallow in your worst season. Most people would love to see you thrown into a pit and not make it to the palace. It's sad but true: there are many who want to see you fail and fall. But when God opens doors for you, and when dreams begin to happen, open your eyes wide. Why? Because the Eliab's in your life will start showing up. They've always been there, but they will begin to speak louder and clearer. David's brother was filled with anger, and his anger was revealed in and through his unnecessary questions: why have you come down here? Your heart will always tell on you. And this moment was no different in David's life. You see, most people don't care about your presence until your presence poses as a problem for them. Most people don't even notice you are there until you can destroy a Goliath that they can't. You've got to have 20/20 vision and focus, and complete every assignment in front of you. David was gifted with the innate ability to destroy what his brothers were afraid of. If he had stopped focusing on Goliath to give attention to Eliab, he would've misappropriated his strength and wasted his energy on someone who was only a distraction.

Oftentimes, gifted people waste their oil on people who are not their enemy. They waste oil on people who are in the family; people who will still be low if you don't rise to the occasion; people who will still complain if you don't change the trajectory of your household; people who are biologically attached to your family and will need you in the next season to deliver them from this one. Keep your focus. The enemy you see today, you won't see forever. But in order to do that, you've got to rise above the criticism. Ignore Eliab. Mute your brothers. Don't be discouraged by their petty questions. To the brothers, David was just a meager shepherd's boy. To them, he was the one responsible for bringing them lunch. But when he slayed Goliath, I'm sure his brothers became even more upset. When he was anointed king, I'm sure his brothers didn't like it. Learn from David and Joseph. You can't control what others don't like about you, but don't let their dislike keep you stagnant and unproductive. Learn how to accept the calling even if it means you will lose some close friendships. Choose the calling over your convenience. Choose the calling over your preference. Choose the calling over your comfort, and God will make sure that your gift will get you out of every prison you happen to find yourself in.

HELP! I WAS DONE WRONG FOR DOING RIGHT
In the highlighted verses that begin this chapter, we are informed of a few critical details about Joseph's current situation. He has been thrown into jail, not for doing something wrong but for doing something right. What do you do when you do right, and you still get treated wrong?

What do you do when you are trying your best to walk in integrity, and you're being falsely accused? How do you respond when you know that someone hates your gift, but you still have love for them? This is Joseph's plight. And, to add insult to injury, he bumps into two people who need their dreams interpreted. Why is it that people still turn to you even when you're in prison? It's because you are gifted. It's because God has equipped you with the grace to help others even when you need help yourself. God has given you a supernatural ability to answer other people's problems, when you still have questions about the problems in your prayer closet yourself.

Ironically, when Joseph went to jail, he was a dreamer. But while he is in jail, he becomes an interpreter. It's not until he enters into solitary confinement that his purpose is upgraded. I wonder what God is trying to upgrade in your life. I wonder what God is trying to develop in your heart. I wonder what change God is trying to bring into your situation, and to make sure it happens, he's employed isolation for the purpose of graduation. I wonder if every dreamer has to endure a season of solitary confinement so that our gifts can grow up. I wonder if we have to experience betrayal, ridicule, and people taking advantage of us so that we can learn how to stop trusting in humans and instead, start trusting in God. Joseph's story is not unlike yours. You have found yourself in seasons and situations that you can't quite figure out. You have found yourself in metaphorical prisons for doing everything right. I'm sure you've cried a few tears, or asked for forgiveness from the very people who hurt you the most. And still, God is using this prison to grow up purpose in you. God is using this scenario to give you a different perspective.

> *God is using this prison to grow up purpose in you. God is using this scenario to give you a different perspective.*

Joseph's gift was enhanced after he submitted to the prison process. Every dreamer has to trust God's process. It may be dark in your prison. It may be lonely in your prison. It may be difficult in your prison. But photos are only developed in the dark room. People are only developed in dark seasons. Great dreamers are only developed in the dark spaces of your life. When people break your heart, that's when you get to see that God is a healer of your emotions. When family members walk away, that's when you see that God is a mother to the motherless. When unemployment hits your house, that's when you learn that God is Jehovah-Jireh. When bills are due and there is no money in your account, that's when you learn to trust God even when you can't trace him.

Your gift is yearning to grow, but sometimes, the only way to grow up in your gift, is to go through in your life. Joseph was in jail for something he didn't do, and while there, he was introduced to two people who needed their dreams interpreted. One biblical character had a good dream. The other had a bad dream. One person died as a result of his dream. The other person lived as a result of his dream. To the one who lived, the chief butler, Joseph asked him to remember him when he got out of prison. The butler promises to remember him while he's in jail, but forgets about him the moment he gets free.

Can you relate to this scenario? Have you ever been used for your gift when someone needed you in their prison, but forgotten about after they decide to move on with their life? Have you ever heard someone promise you the world in the valley, and forget their word in the mountain? Have you ever had someone forget about you? Joseph was forgotten about for two years, until Pharaoh has a dream and stands in need of an interpreter. The butler then remembers his promise to Joseph two years later, and recommends Joseph to the Pharaoh. No one else in the land can interpret his dream. Why? Because when God wants you to come out, he will ensure that every other hindering voice will be silenced until your gift makes room for you. When God wants you to come out, he will allow the brothers who hated on you and the friends who forgot about you, to work for you in the end, because God is sovereign, not their opinion. When God is adamant about you succeeding in life, not even your issues can disqualify you from the next season of your life. This is important because you have to stop looking for your family members to validate who you are. If they don't see your gift, shake the dust and keep it moving.

Jesus said to them, "A prophet is not without honor except in his own town, among his relatives and in his own home." He could not do any miracles there, except lay his hands on a few sick people and heal them. He was amazed at their lack of faith.
Mark 6:4-6

When Jesus saw that people in his home town did not honor him as a prophet and healer, he shook the dust and kept it moving. He never returned to his hometown and he did not perform miracles where there was no faith. In other words, He didn't waste his time trying to prove his power to people who didn't believe in him. Instead, he went to the places where his power was appreciated.

This next season, God is going to introduce you to people and places who appreciate your gift. God is going to remove you from places that tolerate you. You are too anointed to be apologizing for the call of God on your life. You are too gifted to be walking on eggshells every time you enter into the room. God wants to expand his glory in you. He wants to use your gift to change the world. He wants to use your gift to save the very people who forgot about you. So focus on the Giver of the gift, and not the hater of the gift.

Joseph remains in prison for two years, waiting for someone to keep their word. If you wait for people to validate you or liberate you, you'll remain in prison. Trust God to send a dream to Pharaoh that only you can interpret. Trust God to send a problem that only you can solve. If your gift got you in it, your gift will get you out of it.

And Pharaoh said to his servants, "Can we find such a one as this, a man in whom is the Spirit of God?" Then Pharaoh said to Joseph, "Inasmuch as God has shown you all this, there is no one as discerning and wise as you. You shall be over my house, and all my people shall be ruled according to your word; only in regard to the throne will I be greater than you."
Genesis 41:38-40

Joseph didn't know that what others saw as a prison, was in actuality, a conference room. In that space, an exchange of information took place. An exchange of ideas and revelation took place. Joseph was networking and building his relationship base by showing himself friendly to people who seemed beneath him. If you're a gifted person, never allow ego to make you think you are better than someone. The person you are working for now, may end up as your supervisor later. The person you speak to at the receptionist desk, might be the CEO of the company in five years. You never know how God is going to bless you. You never know how God is going to open doors. So you must steward every relationship as if you're talking to the next President of the United States. I know someone who was being considered for a promotion on his job. He was more qualitied for the promotion, but he was not selected for the position. Instead, the company went with the other candidate who had less qualifications. A few months after the other guy received the promotion, he found it difficult to get anything done without going to the guy who should've gotten the position. The person who didn't get the job was the person that the guy relied on to keep his job. And that's how God works sometimes. He may not give you a title, but he will still show you how valuable you are in his eyes, and in the eyes of those who doubt you.

GIFTS WITHOUT WISDOM ARE WASTED

The key to managing this season and managing your gift is wisdom. Wisdom is the principal thing. Joseph had to use wisdom in his management of those key relationships because if he had said or done something to compromise the relationship, he would've never left the prison. Wisdom is important because you need to figure out where to use your gift, and where to allow others gifts to thrive. Many people may pray, "Lord give me a new car," but wisdom will say, "how much can I afford with my new house, this new job, insurance, and my commute to and from work." Wisdom looks at the fine print that your gift doesn't have time to read. Wisdom pays attention to the details that others don't see as important. With every gift you have been given, God has also given you the wisdom to manage that gift effectively. He'll bring people into your life to help you (if you allow them to). He'll bring resources into your life to sharpen and shape you. He won't just leave you out there to fail. For every vision, God will bring provision. And for every student, God will bring a teacher. He loves you too much to see you squander your gift away. He loves you too much to see you cast your pearl to swine. He loves you too much to see you waste time on things that don't matter. Notice that Joseph only interpreted two dreams in prison. He didn't interpret every prisoner who felt like they had a dream. In this season, you've got to know where to expend your energy and where to rest and replenish. You've got to learn how to manage the silent, solitary, suffering moments. You've got to keep your eye on the big picture, and trust God to deliver you at the right time. If Joseph had gotten out of prison a year too soon, or a week too soon, he may have forfeited his opportunity to lead his family. God knows how long you need to stay in your prison to develop your character. And he'll keep you in as long as you need to be there, but he'll also bring you out the moment He sees: you've learned the lesson.

QUESTIONS

1) Identity 3 God-given gifts that you have?

1._____

_____

_____

_____

2._____

_____

_____

_____

3._____

_____

_____

_____

2) How have you sharpened those gifts? If you haven't sharpened those gifts, find a few books that you can read to help you with those gifts, and list the names of the books below?

_____

_____

_____

_____

_____

_____

_____

_____

_____

_____

_____

_____

_____

3) For accountability, determine a timeline of completion below. Where will you go to be trained in your area of gifting? Who will assist you? What information will you read, or what degree will you obtain? A plan will help you to finish.

_____

_____

_____

_____

_____

_____

_____

_____

_____

_____

_____

PRAYER

Below write a prayer of completion. Commit to finishing strong. Commit to learning your craft. Commit to perfection the gift within you.

_____

_____

_____

_____

_____

_____

_____

_____

_____

_____

_____

_____

_____

CHAPTER
Six

I Need the Lord to Give it To Me

Now Joseph had been taken down to Egypt. Potiphar, an Egyptian who was one of Pharaoh's officials, the captain of the guard, bought him from the Ishmaelites who had taken him there. **Genesis 39:1**

Have you ever been on a plane that had to land unexpectedly? Perhaps there was an emergency on the plane, a passenger who took ill, or turbulence in the air, but for whatever reason, the plane had to land without warning, and without your permission. Imagine what the passengers aboard US Airways Flight 1549 felt when they took off on January 15, 2009 from LaGuardia Airport. Everyone was excited. Some people were already asleep. Others were ignoring the flight attendant who was giving the same old instructions they'd heard a million times. Three minutes after take-off, the engine loses its power. A flock of Canadian geese fly overhead at the exact time the plane ascends. The plane strikes these geese to the point that an emergency landing becomes the only option. The pilots were too far away to turn around, and too close to the problem to go above it. So, Chesley Sullenberger and Jeffrey Skiles move on instinct alone.

Not one lesson in the academy can help them right now. They've got to make a quick decision that will save lives or destroy them all. They glide the plane to a soft landing on the Hudson River. There is little time to warn the passengers. They have to move into emergency mode. They have to act now and think later. Because of the decision these two expert pilots made in the heat of a critical moment, no one was hurt. All 155 people aboard the plane were rescued, but their lives changed in the blink of an eye.

Life has a way of shifting in seconds, and if you're not ready for it, you won't know what to do when your engine loses power. Joseph was at home with his family. He was doing what he always does—talking to his brothers about a little dream he had—and then he decided to go find them while they were out hunting or playing, or fishing, or chasing each other. In what seemed like minutes later, Joseph was thrown into a dark pit. Unexpected. From there, he is sequestered and taken captive by people who don't even speak his language. He's working (slaving) in a space that he didn't prepare for. He's living with strangers. He's working and learning at the same time. He went from a free man to a slave boy in seconds. How do you keep dreaming when life snatches the ground out from beneath you?

The answer to that question is the purpose of this chapter. Every dreamer will encounter sudden detours. Every dreamer will interface with a situation that takes them by surprise. But when it happens, you need to know what to do and what not to do. First, understand this: God can use and reconstruct everything he has put in your life to build you into who he wants you to be. The potter knows how to put you back together again. Don't quit because of your past. Don't quit because of the dysfunction in your life. Whenever you place anything in the hands of God, you will succeed. Point. Blank. Period. Don't wait for life to give you the green light. If God says "go," you need to move when He says move. You need to speak when he says speak.

> *Every dreamer will encounter sudden detours. Every dreamer will interface with a situation that takes them by surprise. But when it happens, you need to know what to do and what not to do.*

Joseph didn't let a temporary circumstance stop him

from a permanent blessing. He trusted God every step of the way because he knew something that many of us are still struggling to understand. Firstly, favor is portable. Favor will go with you to your father's house. It will travel with you to Potiphar's house. It will find you in the prison. It will stalk you in the palace. Favor is God's unexplained, undeserved preferential treatment toward you. You can't explain it but it's there. You don't know why, but it's there.

> *Favor is not housed in a coat or a position, because when they stole his coat, they didn't steal Joseph's favor!*

Favor is not housed in a coat or a position, because when they stole his coat, they didn't steal Joseph's favor! When his position changed, he didn't lose his favor. When you are clear about your call, you see that the position may need you but you don't necessarily need the position. Everything you need is wrapped up in your favor. Every door that God will open, will automatically swing open the moment favor meets opportunity. God is giving you thick skin in this season. You'll learning how to walk through every dark valley and declare what David declared; that "yea though I walk through the valley of the shadow of death, I will fear no evil; for thou art with me." I know they left you, but God is with you. I know you are hurting, but God is with you. I know you are waiting for the next opportunity to open up, but God is with you. You are not in this pit alone. You are not in this prison alone. You are not in this meeting alone. You are not on this interview alone. You are not sitting in front of this counselor, or doctor, or judge alone. God is with you. And because God is with you, favor is on you. God wants to show you what it's like to depend on him and only him. It's only when God is all we have that we realize that God is all we need. And in this season, you've got to be willing to dream alone. If Adam didn't go to sleep, Eve wouldn't have come forth. If Jacob didn't send his family away, he would've never had a visitation with God that caused his name, and legacy, to change forever. Sometimes, you are fighting the season of isolation, but there is insulation for your isolation. Your time in this cocoon is helping you to prepare for your wings. Your time as a single person is helping you not to repeat the mistakes you made before. Your time as an only child is giving you the tools to minister to those who are in your shoes. God is working, but are you trusting? God is proving himself, but are your eyes wide open. Joseph still triumphed through every season because he took his eye off of the accoutrements of favor, and began to see the presence of God.

DETOURS WILL HAPPEN

Detours will happen. Unexpected moments will come. But the Lord will give you what to say at the selfsame hour. The Lord will give you what to do at the moment you need to know it. Some people are asking God for success. But what they really need is a strategy. When God gives you a strategy, He gives you plans that will outlast a one-time payment plan. He will give you structure, ideas, people to undergird it, gifts to enhance it, and the big picture beyond what you can see right now. Joseph had a dream, but he had no idea where that dream would take him in the end. In the same way, God only gives us a part of the picture and tells us, "trust me every step of the way." Abraham was destined to become the father of many nations. But God didn't reveal the big picture in the beginning. The first order of business was for Abraham to leave what was familiar in order to embrace change. Once he obeyed the first step, then God revealed the next stage. Once Abraham left the "need" to obey the "call," he was able to see what God had in store for him. In life, you've got to accept that someone will need you in every season of your life. But don't abandon God's call at the expense of man's need. God will fill every void. God will supply what others need. Don't feel guilty about the necessary transition you have to go through. Don't let familiar people keep you stuck in an expired season. You've got to keep it moving. You've got to hear God. You've got to obey his word, even when you can't see "Isaac" or the nations on the first day God speaks.

The same way God spoke to Abraham, and the same way God spoke to Joseph, God is going to lead you beside still waters. He's not going to give you everything you want in the beginning. He's going to wait until you obey step 1 before he reveals step 2. Every dreamer must understand that manifestation requires participation. Faith without works is dead. In order for God to bless you, Joseph, you've got to be willing to interpret dreams in a dingy prison. You've got to be willing to let God use you for two or three. Joseph only spoke to two people in prison, but those people were key figures that pushed him into his next season. Don't wait for the big crowd to give a dynamic word. Live every day as if this might be the moment that God is going to bring about manifestation. Bring your gifts to the table, and work the work of him who sent you while it is day because when night comes, no man can work.

PREPARE FOR THE CHALLENGES

Faith does not come without its challenges. If you can have faith through the difficult times, God will make sure you will win in the end. One year, the church I pastor decided that our focus would be growth. We wanted to grow the people within the church and grow the impact the church was making outside of the walls of our weekly worship service. I had in mind how we would meet this goal of growth, but God was the ultimate decider of the lessons plan. We were excited about all that was going to transpire. We were charged up on several sermons about faith, and we were declaring and decreeing all over the world that God was going to grow us. Well, shortly after our public declaration was made, we got word from our building manager who told us that we had to move out of our church within six months. This couldn't have been a worse time because we were planning for our summer camp at the same time, our discipleship program was growing, and out of nowhere, life happened. The engine stopped. A curve ball appeared. An unexpected turn of events emerged and the people were looking at me and saying, "what now pastor?" What seemed like demise was actually God in disguise. God was answering our prayer. He was growing us, but it didn't look like what we expected. He was growing us in places that we didn't know we needed growth in. He was growing us outside of our comfortable zones of faith. This season caused us to trust him even more. It forced us to think outside of the box. It intensified our prayer life, and it brought our community together.

We started stepping out on faith in a greater way. At that time, all I knew was that I wanted to do something big for God. I knew God had given me vision but I didn't know where the people were going to come from. So I decided, "Lord whatever you give me to do, I will master it." I remembered seeing a video of another church that did an egg drop on Easter Sunday. The idea was simple: invite as many people as possible, and drop eggs out of the helicopter. Inside of those eggs were candy and things for children to enjoy. The egg drop was such a success at that church, they drew thousands of people to their church on a Sunday morning. So I told my team about the idea. I wrote down the plan. I secured five people to assist with the execution of the plan.

I told them, "we're going to drop ten thousand eggs out of a helicopter and thousands of people are going to come." They all looked at me like deer in headlights and said, "Pastor whatever you want, we will do it."

Before I finish this testimony, I need to pause to say this: get around people who will do anything, everything or nothing at all. Find you a few people who will support you until the wheels fall off. Find you a Silas. Find you an Elizabeth. Discover your 12 disciples because everyone in your crowd is not necessary your disciple. Identify your James, Peter, and John—people who will say, "whatever you need, I got you. Whatever you see, I see it, too." Even if they don't see it in the beginning, people who are called to support you will keep on working until the plan is made clear. So we began working. We put out nearly twenty thousand flyers and on the day we held our event, three thousand people showed up! I declared that God was going to do a miracle in our city, and the response was overwhelming and unprecedented!

People from every walk of life showed up. Newspaper journalists showed up. News station commentators showed up, and it was such an outpouring of love for the community. I only had mustardseed faith, but God took what I had and multiplied it to show me that all things are possible to those who believe.

I look back at that moment constantly, and I consistently reminded: "This is what happens when you really, really dream," because the favor of God is not just for pleasure. Favor is a dream gift. Favor is a gift that's designed to make sure that the dream comes into fruition. Favor ensures that your vision will come to pass. I didn't know what one moment would do in our community but God began to blow my mind. After the event happened, pastors from all over the city began to call me. "I can't believe you just did that!" they exclaimed. And at the time, I was twenty five years old, but I could remember pulling into the parking lot and standing in awe of God's miraculous hand. There were so many people at the event, I could not find a parking space myself! Meanwhile, I was the one putting the event on! God's moved in such a tremendous way that now it's become one of our signature events. Every year, people look forward to Easter time, and they flock to our church to enjoy the handiwork of God. We drop ten to twenty thousand eggs from a helicopter and we use it as an evangelistic tool to draw people to Jesus.

> *Favor is a gift that's designed to make sure that the dream comes into fruition.*

While they are there, I preach the Gospel of Jesus before the event happens and hundreds of people come and give their life to God. If you trust God, He will give it to you. He will give you the key to unlock your next door. He will give you the idea to save a generation. He will give you the solution to your community's problem. He will give you the sermon that will incite others to want to know Jesus. He will give you interpretation to get you out of your prison. He will give you the courage to dream again. He will give you the strategy to get out of debt. He will give you the connection to reconcile with your loved ones. He will give you the patience to trust God again. He will give you the hope to endure through difficult seasons. There is nothing too hard for God. If He said it, he will do it. All you have to do is trust him in the shift.

QUESTIONS

1) Name a time when a detour happened in your life that took you out of your comfort zone? What did it teach you about yourself?

_____

_____

_____

_____

_____

_____

_____

_____

_____

_____

_____

_____

2) Are you prepared for life's challenges? Are you prepared for life's detours? How do you know? If you aren't prepared, then what will you do to become prepared?

___
___
___
___
___
___
___
___
___
___
___
___
___
___

PRAYER

Below write a prayer of preparation. Ask God to help you to prepare for the unexpected. Ask him to give you a fresh perspective so that detours don't stop you from destiny.

_____

_____

_____

_____

_____

_____

_____

_____

_____

_____

_____

_____

_____

Manasseh is Coming

"And now let Pharaoh look for a discerning and wise man and put him in charge of the land of Egypt. Let Pharaoh appoint commissioners over the land to take a fifth of the harvest of Egypt during the seven years of abundance.

Before the years of famine came, two sons were born to Joseph by Asenath daughter of Potiphera, priest of On. Joseph named his firstborn Manasseh and said, "It is because God has made me forget all my trouble and all my father's household." The second son he named Ephraim and said, "It is because God has made me fruitful in the land of my suffering." **Genesis 41: 33, 51-52**

Promotion never comes when you expect it. It also never looks like what you thought it would look like. When God wants to bless a dreamer, he will always send his blessing packaged in an unexpected problem. It's a maze of sorts. Have you ever played a videogame like Tetris or perhaps you enjoyed maze puzzles as a kid. The goal was always to get to the open door, but in order to get there, you would have to wind through difficult blockades. Those blockages appeared to be walls in the beginning. But over time, you developed the skill of looking for an unexpected opening. Over time, you trained your brain to calm down and pay attention to the details. If the maze was created, then the creator has designed you to win. In life, especially with dream chasers, you must see every season that way. *If God has you in it, it is because He has equipped you to win.* The wall in front of you may be a financial burden. The wall in front of you might be a health challenge. The wall in front of you might be an age or racial difference, but if God has you in it, it's because He's already orchestrated a way for you to come out of it.

> *If God has you in it, it is because He has equipped you to win.*

Don't stop running the race simply because it doesn't look like you thought it would look like. No one said the road would be easy, but God did promise to be with you even when it doesn't look like He's with you. Abraham didn't think God would intervene on the mountain with his son Isaac, but lo and behold, there was a ram in the bush. The Pharisees and Sadducees of Jesus' day totally missed the Savior because he came wrapped in swaddling clothes. He was their promise on two legs. He was promotion personified. But they missed him, and in fact, crucified him because they thought things would be one way, when God had another plan in mind.

If you're going to be God's dream chaser, you've got to be willing to resign your plans and totally surrender to God's promises. Imagine if Joseph would've allowed his surroundings to alter his perspective? The prison would've eliminated him. The pit would've destroyed him. The betrayal would've overwhelmed him, and the lies would've depressed him. But He knew that God was not unrighteous to forget his labor of love. He knew that the righteous would not be forsaken. He knew that many are the afflictions of the righteous but the Lord will deliver them out of them all. When your winds overwhelm you, and when the threat of life tries to stop you, remember his promises. You may be in prison but recall what God said.

In Genesis 41, we see that God was faithful to bring Joseph out of his predicament, and when he fully delivered him from the misery of his past, he blessed him with two children; one of them being a boy by the name of Manasseh. Manasseh represents the tailor-made blessing that only God can give. Manasseh's name is so important because it helps us to see how God often blesses the dreamer who presses. Manasseh means "to forget." God blessed Joseph with amnesia. That's right. God blessed Joseph with the ability to forget his pain. He blessed him with the ability to forget his sorrow. Joseph was blessed with one child, and that child's presence erased over 30 years of trauma and misery. The same will happen to you if you would just trust the process. *The pain you are in right now is temporary. How do I know? Because there is a Manasseh on the other side of this.* There is a blessing that will cause you to forget how many times you were dropped. There is a promotion that will make you praise God for every minimum wage position. There is a door that God wants to bring you through that will make you forget every rejection letter, every interview that did not result in a job offer, and every school that never responded back to you. When God causes you to forget, he always replaces the pain with a promise. He always fixes your wounds, by forcing you to win. He never leaves you brokenhearted. He will always introduce you to the one he had always had in mind for you. You are not going to die like this. You are not going to cry forever. Weeping may only endure for a night, but joy is going to come in the morning! Your Manasseh is coming. Your healing is coming. Your victory is coming. Your breakthrough is coming. The favor of God is too big in your life for you to wallow in the wilderness of your sadness. God is going to make you forget all of the people that left you, the people that lied on you, and the manipulation that happened. Those time that you were in the pit, those time that you were in the palace, and those times that you were falsely accused, Manasseh represents a bridge in your life. Before the bridge, you were in one place. After the bridge, you were in another place. Without the bridge, you would've likely drowned in the water, or fallen into a bottomless pit. But God creates bridges called "Manasseh" to help you remember where your pain stopped and God's blessings began. Joseph endured for decades, and one child being born changed everything for a lifetime. I wonder what dream God wants to birth in you that will change the trajectory of your entire life. I wonder what book God wants you to write that will cause you to forget all of the stuff you had to endure to write it. I wonder what position God has in your future that will cause you to forget. You may be bent out of shape over a relationship that failed. But God is going to cause you to forget. He's not just going to let you forget what happened to you; he's also going to let you forget the pain that's associated with it.

FORGIVE AND FORGET

You have heard it said many times that in order to move forward, you have to "Forgive and forget." In fact, there used to be a television talk show with that very title—forgive and forget. But how possible is it to really forgive a person if you have forgotten what they did? What do you do with the wounds that won't go away, and the memories that won't erase from your mind—even when you're trying to move on. I believe God uses Manasseh's birth to teach us how to answer that question. When God is telling you to forget, he's not telling you to forget the lesson you learned because of it. He's telling you to forget the grudge you were holding in spite of it. He's telling you take the meat and throw out the bone. Let go of anything that is binding you to a previous season that no longer defines who you are. Forget that! Forgive because you have learned a lesson, and as a result, you are wiser. As a result, you are better. As a result, you are stronger. As a result, you are more focused. When God causes you to forget, the memories won't master you, and the lessons will only graduate you. So take the lesson, throw away the pain.

> *When God causes you to forget, the memories won't master you, and the lessons will only graduate you.*

Take the promotion. Throw away the problem. Every season leading up until this moment was a seed of God's wisdom. He was using it to push you into your next level of greatness.

WISDOM IS THE PRINCIPAL THING

Have you ever seen a gifted person who was more talented than they realized? Or, better said, have you ever seen a wealthy person who couldn't manage the riches they were given? As a result, they squandered what they had received, like the Prodigal Son, in riotous living. Or, they spent money on things they didn't need, all because they have the tools but not the wisdom to utilize those tools correctly. The worst thing a dreamer could ever do is have wonderful gifts without practical wisdom. It's never a good thing to have more gift than understanding. Hence, sometimes God will give us a great gift—like He gave to Joseph-but we don't have the wisdom to manage it. Joseph was a dreamer and an interpreter. His gift was greater than his management, so God allowed certain situations to build up stamina and character within him. In the same way, God may be using situations in your life to build up character and stamina within you. To prevent unnecessary pits, prisons, and Potiphars, ask God for wisdom. Ask God for guidance. Jesus said to come to him all who are weary. Come to Jesus when you're weary. Come to him when you're excited. Acknowledge him in all of your ways, and ask him to direct your steps. The Bible also says, "If any man lacks wisdom, ask and He will freely give." God is not holding wise counsel hostage. He isn't selling divine principles to the highest bidder. Sometimes the reason we can't use our gift properly is because we're not talking to the one who created that gift. We need to go to the Manufacturer for instructions on the product he made; only God knows the proper method and process needed to sustain your blessing. Wisdom is the principal thing. Sometimes, dreamers don't need more skills; they just need more wisdom. Sometimes we don't need to run to experts in our field; we just need to run to the book of Proverbs in our Bible.

Proverbs is one of several books that comprise what most historians call Wisdom Literature in Scripture. In Proverbs, the writer uses multiple verses to ensure that the believer understands the necessity of wisdom. Let me break it down for you. Wisdom is not an added feature. Wisdom is not a bonus perk. Wisdom is the engine that drives your dream. Wisdom is the fertilizer that grows your faith. Without wisdom, your car does not have a driving wheel. Your gift may be the head of your body, but wisdom is the neck. If you don't employ wisdom, your vision will file for bankruptcy sooner than you realize. Wisdom isn't something we should wake up thinking about (that's not realistic), but it is something we should ask for.

WISDOM THROUGH EXPERIENCE

Some wisdom happens through education. Other wisdom is received by experience. Some wisdom will be ascertained from listening to others, paying attention to their pitfalls, and avoiding traps. Other wisdom is developed within you because the situation taught you what to do and what not to do. As a new pastor, I remember looking for an organ for our second-year celebration service. I was looking high and low for this organ, and I didn't have much luck in the beginning. But eventually a pastor called me. This particular pastor had just finished speaking at my church and I asked him, "Do you know anyone who might be selling an organ?" When he called me, he said, "Yeah, I'm selling one." I told him that I'd like to buy it from him and he said, "Okay $5,000." I went to him and brought him what he had asked for: $5,000. It was $5,000 cash from my personal monies, and lo and behold, to this day I still have not received that organ. I was relying on him to keep his word because he was a pastor. I assumed that my integrity was his integrity. He was effective when he came to preach, so I thought, "If you can preach like that, certainly you have the gift of God inside of you." Surely, the man of God would not deceive me out of $5,000. That situation taught me something. I gained wisdom that I didn't have before. I learned a valuable lesson that I thought I knew, but I had never been tested in. Before I ever make a purchase (especially one of that magnitude), I need to ask God and then vet the person. I lost out big time, but God taught me to ask better questions, and to get proof before purchase. I learned how to put down a deposit until delivery of the promised product, and to never assume that because someone claims to be a pastor or a Christian, that they will be any less duplicitous than another (all because of a title). I could blame that pastor all day for what he did to me, but the truth is, I didn't acknowledge God in all of my ways. I didn't pray. I assumed. I saw what I wanted, and I stepped out on impulse.

If you're going to gain wisdom from the last season, then you can't blame the devil for your impulsiveness. You can't blame your family members for things that had nothing to do with them. Own up to your own faults. Be honest about things you could've done differently, and allow God to use this situation as experience to help you avoid future calamity and dissatisfaction.

GENERATIONAL BLESSINGS AND GENERATIONAL CURSES

Joseph was the son of Jacob. Jacob was the son of Isaac. Isaac was the son of Abraham. All of these men struggled with deception. Abraham lied and pretended his wife was his sister. Isaac lied and pretended his wife was his sister as well. Jacob lied and pretended to be Esau so he could get the blessing of the firstborn. And Joseph was the son of all of this deception. He marinated in a toxic womb. There were generational blessings on his life because Abraham was the father of many nations. But there were also generational curses on his life. If Joseph didn't learn to identify what was on him, then he would have inevitably birthed more children like the stuff he inherited.

Every dreamer must know what rests in your bloodline. What pathologies and tendencies exist in your entire family? What keeps popping up, and now, you know it's more than mere coincidence? Certainly, Jesus has washed us from all sin by his blood, but we still have our parent's DNA. We still have cells in our body that trace back to what we come from. One family can have a generational curse of sickness and disease. There may be certain illnesses that follow your family down several generations before you. Without knowing what's in your family, you could be squandering your favor and subjecting yourself to unnecessary peril. No matter how anointed Isaac was, he was formed in a family of deception. In order to avoid deceiving others, he had to recognize the patterns and make an alternative choice. What patterns keep popping up in your family? What attitudinal dispositions keep reoccurring in your lineage? Is everyone passive-aggressive in your household? Do you all have a problem with keeping a budget? Are you given to depression for seemingly no reason? Is lust pervasive in your household? Have you ever asked your parents why they divorced, or why your grandparents divorced before them? Jesus has the power to break every curse, but until you recognize the patterns, you are still under its diabolical influence.

DON'T COMPROMISE YOUR FAVOR

You may be compromising your favor and not even know it. There are some families that have a generational curse or a generational habit of infidelity. The dad cheated on the mom, then the son cheated on his wife and the granddaughter cheated on her husband. A generational curse is something that has permission to continue until someone decides to stop it. With the favor of God, you've got to make sure that you don't have these things in you that contaminate your favor. Joseph used one season of birthing (Manasseh) to declare an end to the curses of his past. He declared, "no more to deception," and he refused to be what his brothers and father had been to him. He refused to lie to his brothers when they came before him begging in the end. He disclosed his true self, and that broke him away from the deception he was raised in.

> *God wants to do more than dream through you. He wants to destroy strongholds in your family.*

God wants to do more than dream through you. He wants to destroy strongholds in your family. He wants to use you to change your community. He wants to use you to change your nation. He did not give you all of these gifts so you could hide them under a bushel. He gave you these gifts so you could shift the atmosphere. He gave you these gifts so you could create a new paradigm. Identify what has been holding you and your family back. Then pray for divine intervention. Pray that God will bind the strongman. Pray that God will deliver you and your family from the evil one. If you don't get delivered, you will contaminate your favor. If you don't get free from the grips of the sin you inherited, you will self-sabotage your future.

SELF-SABOTAGING TENDENCIES

Have you ever met someone who can't keep a job? No matter who they work for, and no matter how much the salary pays, after 3-4 months, they are back out on the job search again. This may not be the supervisor's fault. This may not be a procedural problem at work. This may be an example of self-sabotaging behavior that is showing up in the inability to commit long-term.

If you can't commit to anything, then you can't commit to everything. The lack of commitment may be destroying your harvest.

If you can't commit to anything, then you can't commit to everything. The lack of commitment may be destroying your harvest. Your attitude may be destroying future opportunities for you. Nobody wants to hire someone who is mean and unreasonable all of the time. If you're always mismanaging your funds, then you'll never be able to stock up on your finances. Don't contaminate your blessing because you never learned how to budget. Take a class. Ask for help. Go to therapy. Whatever you need to do, allow God to show you how to manage this next season properly.

I believe every season of Joseph's life, was necessary to teach him something new. He was learning how to be a better person, a better steward, a better leader, and now a better father. With the birth of Manasseh God was using every episode to strengthen the areas that remained. Imagine if Joseph had become offended by God for a season that God had already delivered him from? Imagine if Joseph had decided to hold onto pain that had already been relieved and rectified, while living in the palace? How many times do we do that—we go through a tough season and then when relief comes, we still drag the trauma of our past season into the current reality of our present season? In other words, we leave Egypt. We sojourn through the wilderness, and when we get to Canaan, we start blaming Canaan for what Egypt did to us. When we finally break free from the stronghold of yesterday, we blame our past and stay stuck in our misery.

Meanwhile, God has turned the page. He has caused others to forget, but you won't let it go.

In my early 20s, I remember going through a period in my life where it seemed like every one had disappeared. Everyone I considered a friend, had disappeared. For the life of me I could not understand why God would allow that to happen. But now I know: it was God trying to use that "disappearing act" to help me understand that I cannot rely on anyone more than Him. I couldn't put my trust in others. I had to put my trust in God alone.

Later, as months, weeks and years passed by, I started to appreciate the process He put me through. The solitude in one season ensured my success in another season. I wanted human company but I didn't want those humans to captivate me. I didn't want them to show up for me in one season and then disappear in the next; ultimately causing me to feel a seesaw of emotions. God wanted me to learn to depend on him and him alone. And there is no way you can do that with voices and other people around you 24/7. After I learned the lesson and gained the maturity necessary to handle friends, God blessed me with a few trusted dream-carriers. Just a few. And when He blessed me, I didn't hold a grudge. I didn't put up a wall (just in case things didn't work out). I opened myself up to the people God brought into my life, and I never let those people distract me from Him.

For every Dreamer reading this book, I want you to know that Manasseh is coming. If Manasseh hasn't already come, he is on the way. Relief is coming. Freedom is coming. Deliverance is coming. Joy is coming. A new season is coming. A new reason to smile is coming. Don't live in the pit. Don't swim in the prison. Don't reside in the pain. Don't dwell in the foolishness. Keep looking for God to bring you into a season that you will never forget, because He has caused you to forget the pain in order to bring you into prosperity. Out with the old…in with the new!

QUESTIONS

1) Since Wisdom is the principal thing, identify 3 scriptures that help you to remain wise in life?

1._____

2._____

3._____

2) What does Manasseh represent in your life? How do you believe God is going to bring change in your life?

3) What are the generational curses and blessings in your family? How have they impacted you?

PRAYER

In the space below, pray for a new beginning. Ask God to help you to learn the lesson as He removes the pain.

_____

_____

_____

_____

_____

_____

_____

_____

_____

_____

_____

_____

_____

CHAPTER
Eight

I Need to Reset

"Even now," declares the Lord,
"return to me with all your heart,
with fasting and weeping and mourning."
Rend your heart
and not your garments.
Return to the Lord your God,
for he is gracious and compassionate,
slow to anger and abounding in love,
and he relents from sending calamity.
Who knows? He may turn and relent
and leave behind a blessing — **Joel 2:12-14**

When our church first started, I was 22 years old. I remember people saying things like, "Aww, that little 22-year-old boy. What does he know? What is he doing? He can't teach us anything." It was a very unfavorable situation. I didn't like that people underestimated my calling because of my age. I didn't like that people had an opinion about my success before they even gave me a chance to prove myself. I felt like Jeremiah; called to speak as a child but I didn't necessarily have the support of the people around me. Have you ever had a God-sized dream in you, and haters around you? Even if they weren't hating, any act of non-support is a commitment not to support. Any word of negativity during a season of initiation can be devastating. But still, I pressed on. I had a word from God, a promise from God, and a people who had a mind to work. I couldn't be distracted by the people who weren't there. I had to focus my energy on the people who were there. As the years went on, we grew and grew and grew. Despite the odds, we kept growing. Despite my age, we kept growing; because when God starts a thing, He's faithful to complete it.

At present, we are a church on whom our local community depends. Every summer, we have 50 kids, from the streets, who are enrolled in our summer program. Our church has become a beacon of light and hope in our community. We began in an unfavorable position. We began with critics saying that this young boy didn't know what he was doing, but now we are a resource to the community. I want you to know that it does not matter how you start. God wants you to keep moving until you see the promise being fulfilled. You are a finisher. You were born to complete what He began in

> *Don't let the criticism of one stop you from changing the lives of thousands.*

you. Don't let the criticism of one stop you from changing the lives of thousands. Don't let the embryonic stages of formation dissuade you from destiny. All of us have to start somewhere. All of us need a reminder so that when we stand in the need of a revival, we can look back and see what God has brought us from.

MY STORAGE IS EMPTY

At some point, your dream fluid is going to run out. At some point, you will get tired. But you need to chronicle as many memories as possible, to keep you inspired during the difficult seasons. Now that I'm older, I often think about what I would've done differently at 22 years old. If I was talking to myself, I would tell the 22-year-old version of me, "Xavier, never get caught up in the crowd. Always preach, lead and minister what the people need—Jesus." I know it seems like a simple point but you'd be surprised by how many preachers will cater to people's wants and not give them what they need. At the end of the day, what we need is Jesus. If you're a dreamer, you need Jesus. If you're a builder, you need Jesus. If you're rich, poor, healthy, sick, a bishop or an usher, you need Jesus. Jesus has to be at the center of everything, or else it will not work. People will start to depend on you, instead of depending on God. People will become attached to you instead of being attached to God. I've met many people like that. They are easily identified these days. When people are attached to a person and not to a mission, they will give you problems no matter what. You'll recognize these dream blockers when you have a big leap of faith happening, and they are defiant and non-compliant. They will either fold or they will complain. When our church dreamed up the egg drop initiative, there were many who said they were 100% committed to the vision. They were in support of it. But after the event, we never saw them again. Their motive was for attention. They wanted to be seen. They had enough faith for an event but not enough faith to make an impact. Be careful of people who try to zap your joy by becoming selective project-oriented builders. Don't let temporary people take up permanent space. Create boundaries so that they don't drain you and destroy your joy.

TRUST IN GOD ALONE

I have learned too many times to count, the importance of trusting in God. People will abandon you. People will leave you. But God will never leave. God will never destroy you. When I needed revival the most, was when I felt abandonment.

In seasons where I needed to be refreshed, were often the same seasons where I felt the most depressed, alone, and overwhelmed. Abandonment will cause you to ask questions of God. I remember saying to him, "God did you call me to this? If so, then where is the reinforcement? Where is my help?" God reminded me, "I am the reinforcement." With me, there are more for you than against you. I am the God who brings cohesion. I am the God who supports vision. I am the God who makes the impossible possible. Abandonment is a reminder that God is always on your side. I can't tell you how many verses I've read where Jesus found himself abandoned. Thousands followed him while he was feeding them, and healing them, but when it came time for them to take up their cross and deny themselves, the people who were once there were now nowhere to be found. If you constantly subject yourself to the applause or approval of people, you will always be bound by that. You will always need people to refresh you. You will always depend on people to help you initiate what ever it is that you have set out to do. Rise above the crowd. Pursue Christ. When you get to Him,

> *If you constantly subject yourself to the applause or approval of people, you will always be bound by that.*

revival can begin. When you reach Christ, transformation can be sustained. When you determine to focus on Christ, then people's rejection won't hurt as much. People's denial won't bother you as much. The only way to break co-dependency is to change the source of your dependents. Depend on God because it's impossible for him to fail. Failure is not in his vocabulary. Depend on God because He will push you to keep dreaming. He will inspire you to locate and identify, "goers." Every dreamer needs to go with people who are willing to go. You don't have time to beg for company. You need to pursue covenant. Somebody's always going to be willing to go. Somebody will always say they are going, and then turn back. God knows who will go and who will turn away. But don't stop your momentum because the returners didn't stay. Focus on the goers. Not the returners. Focus on Ruth, not Orpah. Focus on Peter, not Judas. Focus on the ones who stayed and not the ones who left.

I believe this was why God cut Gideon's army down. I'm sure Gideon thought that he needed all of those people but he ended up with 300. The number 300 is different for everybody. 300 might mean 40 for me. 300 might mean 10 for someone else. But the point is: if you're going to pursue God's dream in you with all of your mind, then you've got to determine to go with the people that are willing to go with you. Be confident that if God called you to it, He will use the stamina and the strength of those that are going to push the vision forward.

LORD, SEND A REVIVAL

Along the journey, you will get tired. You will get overwhelmed. You will get discouraged. That's a natural part of the process. All of us will go through this. Everybody will need a reset at some point. Everyone will need to recalibrate. Computers have to reset to ensure that the hard drive doesn't crash. Television shows have to reset so that they can prepare for the next season. In the same way, every dreamer needs to reset. In church, we call this a revival. You may be in need of a revival if and when you feel burnt out by the thing that used to replenish you. You may be in need of a revival if the workload is great but your joy is low. You may need a revival if you are working harder than you are resting. If you aren't managing the dream well with other responsibilities, then that may be a clue that you need a reset. If you have become mean and irritable with the people who are called to help you, then you need to reset. Jesus knew the power of a reset. He would often disappear into a solitary place to recharge.

He was a healer. He was a teacher. But he was also human. Sometimes you don't need to quit, you just need a vacation. Sometimes you need to steal away for a moment and get in God's presence. There is nothing wrong with resetting in the presence of the Lord.

The absence of revival is famine. The absence of revival is a drought. God did not build you to work non-stop. You need to take healthy breaks. Perhaps this is why God implemented the Sabbath in Genesis—not because God needed rest but because we need rest! God created a model for us to pattern our lives by. God used the seventh day to show you the importance of resetting, recalibrating, refreshing, and unplugging. You can't operate the way God wants you to operate without proper rest. When Adam rested, Eve was created. I wonder what God can birth in you while you are sleeping that he can't do through you while you are overworking? Rest and revival are essential tools of refreshing for every dreamer. Joseph was in prison for two years, and it may have appeared to be punishment. But looking back at the story, what if it was God putting in two years of rest because he knew that in the next season of his life, he wouldn't have time to sit around and do nothing? Failure to rest will result in bad habits becoming normal life patterns.

IF YOU DON'T STOP, GOD WILL STOP YOU!

I met a young lady when I came home from college. A man of God had introduced me to her. I think I told her, "You're going to be my wife." I was 19 years old. I saw that she was "available" so I assumed she was my wife. Later I learned that lo and behold, just because something is available doesn't mean that it is your destiny. So God arranged for that relationship to fall apart. He destroyed my plans so that His purpose could come to pass. Looking back, I realize now that if I had married her, it would have been a major problem. I didn't want to turn 30 without a wife, but I also didn't want to get a divorce by 30. God stopped me and showed me that I was turning to people for something that I could only get from Him. I was looking at this young lady and assuming she was called to me because she was available, but God was telling me that it wasn't the right time for that. Sometimes, you can have the right thing in the wrong season. Sometimes, you can have the right job but in the wrong season. You've got to discern the times so that you aren't falling in love with an expired season. If you don't stop yourself, God will stop you. If you don't humble yourself, God will humble you! I heard somebody say, "How you do anything is how you do everything." So if you approach your horizontal relationships from a broken place, then you will approach your vertical relationship with God from a broken place. I think it's valuable that we go to God for proper healing so that we can exude healing in our horizontal relationships.

> *When you understand what revival truly is, then you can set your life on a trajectory of wholeness and breakthrough.*

I needed God to heal me before I tried to love anyone else. I needed God to refresh me in his presence before I submitted myself to someone else's. What do you need God to do that you are looking for others to do? What in your life needs repair from His presence that you've been trying to rectify in others? Every season of your life was ordained to strengthen your dream. Every season was meant to empower your purpose. When you understand what revival truly is, then you can set your life on a trajectory of wholeness and breakthrough.

REVIVAL 101

Obviously, revival is not a shout or a praise break. But it's a move of God that causes God to wake up that which was dead. God wants to wake up our passions. God wants to wake up our dreams. God wants to wake up our understanding. Revival moments are necessary because if God is going to release favor on you (but you're too tired to receive it or you are too dysfunctional and your perception is off), then you'll take that favor and mismanage it. We all need a reset and it comes by prayer and fasting. But don't assume that you can do this alone. Identify people around you who can hold you accountable. Find people that know and detect Jesus. Connect with people who will tell you the truth. You need people who will tell you, "Listen, I'm noticing something. You're not as responsive as you used to be." Or "You're now starting to complain a lot." Or, "you're now starting to get aggravated and frustrated quite frequently." You need to have someone around you that can recognize your habits and your proclivities. With accountability, you have an opportunity to catch yourself before you're too far gone. And most of the time, we don't know that we need revival until it's too late. But this season is reversible. I believe you are reading these words on time. You have the tools, but tools with no zeal will leave you powerless. Instructions without desire will leave you fruitless.

    As a pastor, I've had many married couples come in and sit across the table and point at each other and say,

"She's the problem. No. He's the problem. No. The kids are the problem." They're pointing fingers at other things but not really acknowledging and taking account for themselves. That happens when people don't realize Hey, I need a reset. Yes, I am jaded. Yes, some things are off. But I can't blame anyone else. I have to own up to my own issues. I haven't been praying as often. I haven't been in my Word as much. The beginning of your new season will begin when you admit, "God I need a reset." Like David said, 'Create in me a clean heart and renew a right spirit within me'." It becomes detrimental or deadly to any relationship if you don't get your heart checked. It's awful when relationships are struggling because one person is exhausted and the other is hopeful. Children are impacted. Finances are impacted. The church is impacted. Everything is impacted. But it's not too late to turn this around. Ask God to fill you with His presence. Ask Him to reconnect you to His power and presence. Shift from a place of apathy to a place of surrender. Don't let the enemy win. You are stronger than this. You are better than this. You can do all things through Christ who is our strength. Go! Get your joy back! Your next level of dream impartation is depending on you to surrender to the reset.

QUESTIONS

1) What are some signs that you may need a reset?

2) What are you going to do to reconnect with God?

3) What are you going to do to reconnect with God?

PRAYER

Below, write a prayer for revival. Ask God to refocus you, re-center you, and refresh you in His presence.

_____

_____

_____

_____

_____

_____

_____

_____

_____

_____

_____

_____

_____

It Didn't Kill Me

When Joseph arrived at Shechem, a man found him wandering around in the fields and asked him, "What are you looking for?" He replied, "I'm looking for my brothers. Can you tell me where they are grazing their flocks?" "They have moved on from here," the man answered. "I heard them say, 'Let's go to Dothan.'" So Joseph went after his brothers and found them near Dothan. But they saw him in the distance, and before he reached them, they plotted to kill him.
Genesis 37:14-18

The most dangerous prayer that I ever prayed this year was this: "God, I'm ready to grow. So please grow me." I was ready to grow personally. I was ready to grow the people and I was ready to grow the church. I thought I was going to get to choose which lessons I was going to learn.

> *When you tell God, "I'm ready to grow," He chooses the lessons and He chooses the teacher.*

I thought I was going to dictate how growth would look in my life. But I've learned the hard way: When you tell God,

"I'm ready to grow," He chooses the lessons and He chooses the teacher. I thought I was stagnated, but God had my life on pause for a reason. I now know that if the production had kept going, and I was still the person I was, I would've destroyed the whole production. Every season of Joseph's life was purposeful. Even when he felt shame, embarrassment, delay, and frustration it was on purpose. His isolation brought insulation. His prison brought promotion. I was ready to grow, but I didn't expect the course God was going to take me on.

August of 2017 was life-changing for me. I went to church one Sunday, preached and had a few meetings. I was preparing my mind for work the next day when my friend called me and said, "Hey, I'm going to the beach." I said, "You know what, I have to catch up on some reading so I think I'm going to join you. My car is having some trouble so I'll ride with you." It took a minute for him to text me back, but when he did he said, "Sure, it's ok for you to ride with me *and my friend.*" I didn't know he was going with another person, so I responded with these words: to be honest, I don't really like hanging out with people I don't know. I'm not a crowd's guy." To which my friend replied, "You need to quit acting like that and come on with us." So reluctantly, I decided to go with my friend and my friend's friend. I went to my house and changed clothes.

When I got there, my friend texts me and says, "we're outside." I come outside and get in the car. We're ready to go to the beach, but the friend of my friend wanted to stop in Brownsville to pick up his friend. I didn't feel right about it, but we drove into the neighborhood anyway. The area was a nice neighborhood; it looked like my mom's neighborhood. I remember the house we stopped at because it didn't have a fence, and I'm accustomed to remembering my surroundings in case of an emergency.

The day was great. We went to the beach, and we were having a great time. I'm relaxing, reading and enjoying the weather. I take a few pictures and we decide to leave and go eat at Applebee's. I don't prefer Applebee's but I didn't want to be a party pooper. I also didn't drive so I had to comply. So, we went to Applebee's.

Done for the evening. We are on our way back from Applebee's and the beach. We have to return to Brownsville to drop off the friend of my friend. We roll down the street and I see four people sitting in the yard. The lights are off but it looks just like my mom's house. There are cars in the yard. I thought these people were getting ready to walk their guests to their cars. We stopped in front of the house and I see a guy move to get out. He points his arms in the direction of our car. But there was something in his hand—it looks like a gun—it is a gun. And then I see them motion toward the car. All I can say is, "Nooooo" in what felt like slow motion. The person who was in the back of the car started yelling, "No, it's me!" I looked down and I felt something warm. Then I screamed, "I'm shot! I'm shot! I'm shot!"

I could not hear any bullets. I told my friend, "Take your shirt off or I will be dead in 180 seconds." The blood was gushing so much, I thought it hit my femoral artery. My life flashed in front of me. All I could do was say, "The blood of Jesus!" As I kept saying it, I didn't know where I was, but I saw everything moving fast. Sweat began to pour down my face. I felt myself going into shock. We turned and made a wrong turn (which was really a right turn) in a parking lot. As we were coming out of the parking lot, a rescue truck was waiting for me. I told them to do whatever they had to do to get to the rescue truck. I jumped out with blood gushing everywhere. I told them to help me. I told them who I was. He took me and put me on a stretcher, and said, "You've been shot. The bullet went through both of your legs. We don't know where else you've been shot, but we've got to cut everything off of you." They gave me IV fluids. They did everything they could to stabilize me. I was telling them to tell my family I love them. I told them I knew God was with me. I didn't know if I should've been crying, laughing, or screaming. All I knew was that I needed to get to the hospital as the blood was pouring and pouring and pouring. When I got to the trauma center, seven or eight doctors surrounded me. I asked them to keep me conscious, and they told me that was the least of my worries. They took an x-ray and discovered that the bullets didn't hit any bones. I was hit with a high caliber weapon. The bullet came through the door, hit both legs with the same level of power, and hit an ash tray without hitting anyone else.

When I got to CT, the surgeon walked up to me and said, "You, my friend, are blessed." I looked at him and told him, "Yes I know." The surgeon explained that the bullet went through the muscle only, and because it didn't hit a major organ, he could discharge me on the same day. He said, "You must have work to do, because someone is looking out for you." I corrected him and said, "God." It was nobody but God that kept me that day, and all I can say is…thank God… *it didn't kill me.*

Now what's amazing is this: I had finished writing this book before this incident happened. The title of this chapter was already "It Didn't Kill Me." But I had no clue how accurate this title was to my life. I had no clue that Joseph was my life's story and that God was still writing it. I knew God wanted me to encourage the dreamer in you, but I didn't know that God was going to use my life to encourage the dreamer in me. I want to remind you through my testimony, that God will sustain you. God will keep you alive until you accomplish what He put you in the earth to do. You are not finished yet. God is still working. You are not done yet. God has plans for you to accomplish. I can't tell you how being shot changed my entire perspective but it gave me a new lease on life. It helped me to push past fear, push past nervousness, push past questions, and just do all that God told me to do.

Joseph's brothers wanted to kill Joseph before he walked into his greatest season. Joseph wasn't even where he was going to be yet. But they wanted to kill him before his potential manifested. The Bible says they had seen him coming from a distance. So he still hadn't made it to where they were. But the fact that they saw him coming led them to stop him before he got there. The enemy is going to plot and plan. But it's not going to kill you. The enemy is going to take you down streets you didn't want to go on. But it's

CHAPTER NINE | 159 |

not going to kill you. The enemy is going to shoot you with a bullet that was supposed to hurt someone else. But it's not going to kill you. It's going to help you. So, if you take the life of Joseph and look at it in perpetuity, you will see: that the trials in his life only made him stronger. It didn't kill him although it was designed to destroy him.

PRAISE GOD IT DIDN'T KILL YOU

There is a point of celebration that must take place whenever we arrive to any level of progress. We need to celebrate the small things because there is always some level of opposition designed to stop us. Whether that is growing up in an impoverished home. Whether that is being in a dysfunctional relationship. Whether we have battled with mental issues or health issues. There is always something that is designed to intentionally trap us or kill us. And not necessarily kill us from a physical place but kill our drive and kill our passion. So we've got to learn to celebrate the small victories.

> *if you take the life of Joseph and look at it in perpetuity, you will see: that the trials in his life only made him stronger.*

I am learning now to celebrate life. I am learning to

celebrate health. I am learning to celebrate something as simple as dressing myself, and walking to the kitchen. God didn't have to spare my life, and when you are in a position where the enemy could've taken your life and God blocked it, it resurrects hope. It changes your praise. You stop asking for things and start thanking Him for what He's already done. God is faithful. His promises are sure. Celebrate the small victories until you win the entire race. Celebrate the tests you pass until you graduate with the degree you want. Celebrate the fact that you didn't go off on your boss, and watch God promote you in due season. Celebrate what God has already done and it will empower you to see what He is going to do! He is not finished with you yet. You can't give up now. It may be hard, but God is going to help you to finish everything you've started.

When I first desired to get my Master's degree, I had a lot of people around me saying things like, "Why are you going back to school? Don't you know you will accrue more debt?" You don't need that. That's not going to work for you.

CHAPTER NINE

That's not going to change anything. That's just extra work for nothing. They saw me coming. They saw my passion. They saw my desire to go higher and to get deeper in my education. But instead of encouraging me, they found every reason to discourage me. They filled my mind with reasons why it couldn't work and wouldn't work. They found every reason to tell me why I couldn't do it. Although I could appreciate their concern about loans, I would have preferred if they said, "You're going to have loans. But you can do this. The way the world is moving, you've got to be educated. Xavier, get your degree, you need this for where you aspire to be." But instead I didn't get that. I got negativity. I got unnecessary dialogue. I got brothers who were hating on me and wanted to kill my hope before it lifted from the ground. But God is my strength. He is my counselor when I need encouragement. He is my completion and my ammunition. I turn to him for strength. I turn to him for courage. I turn to him for a Word. He is my present help in the time of trouble. If God could spare my life from the accident I was in, surely God could

> *God is my strength. He is my counselor when I need encouragement. He is my completion and my ammunition.*

help me finish this degree. Surely God will be with me as I grow His church. Surely, God will meet every financial need that comes my way.

LET GO AND LET GOD

One of the greatest lessons I've learned in this season is this: you don't always have to be right. You don't always have to be in control. You can forgive. You can give grace where you need grace. And if you want the other person to forgive you, then you must forgive them. Anything less than that, is dysfunctional. I can't want Joseph's blessings and not forgive Joseph's brothers.

> *I can't want Joseph's blessings and not forgive Joseph's brothers.*

In any relationship, there should be reciprocity. It's a give and take. If you don't have reciprocity, then what you have is dysfunction. There can't be a flow if things are clogged up. There can't be cohesion if everything is one-sided. No matter what Joseph's brothers do to you, keep your heart clear of dysfunction. Do what's right so that dysfunction doesn't fester and reign. If you're not careful, dysfunction will start as an ant and end as a bear. It will continue to grow. It is like a cancer. It doesn't just come into one place. It starts scattering to every place. It will start spilling over into your workplace. People won't even be comfortable working with you at work. It will spill over in your home. Your husband or your wife will feel uncomfortable with being in connection with you. The people in church will start getting agitated because they will start seeing signs of this dysfunction. It will start spilling into every part of your life. Before you know it, dysfunction will become a bear that will consume you and have you hostage without you knowing it. You have to be careful.

The situations that happened in my life were intended to make me bitter. They happened so I would be paranoid and full of resentment. But God taught me how to live beyond the enemy's desire to kill me. I had to be free from this dysfunction and hold onto my dream. I had to step up my game as it relates to my spiritual/devotional life. The only way that we can identify dysfunction is if we have a relationship with God. God's word is the original blueprint. Once we recognize something is off, we need start praying. Ask yourself, *Is this something I can modify or do I need God to modify it?* If it's something that we can do, then do it. If it's something that only God can do, then learn to cooperate with God so that God can manifest Himself. Don't get bent out of shape over things you can't control. You cannot control how other people perceive you but you can control how you react. Reacting with some level of integrity is important. I could not control the people who shot me. But I could control how I reacted when I saw them again. I couldn't control the negative comments from people who discouraged me from going back to school. But what I could control was my invitation letter to my graduation celebration. What Joseph's brothers didn't understand is that God was going to bless Joseph with or without them. God didn't say he would bless Joseph exclusively. In other words, He didn't say He wasn't going to bless the brothers. But resentment will only let you see the part of the story that makes you bitter. They came up with their own concept thinking that they weren't going to be blessed because Joseph got blessed. So in that case you can't consume yourself trying to prove to other people or correct them or coddle their misinterpretation of what God is doing. You've got to be consistent in your vision, your passion and your dream. Let God bring clarity to their misinterpretation.

At the end of the day, you are Joseph for a reason. You have been called to greatness. You have been called to shift your family. You have been called to bless those who curse you. You have been called to dream and interpret dreams. You have been called to help those who hurt you. You have been called to chase after and accomplish every single thing God has put in your heart to do. So if you're reading this, that means you're still alive. If you can turn the pages of this book, then that means it didn't kill you. The weapon was formed but it did not prosper. The enemy came in like a flood, but the spirit of the Lord lifted up a standard. It did not work! It did not prosper. God has won the victory, and you are going to win the war! This is all working together for your good. Work now! Celebrate later. Welcome to your next level of dream chasing!

QUESTIONS

1) Which chapter spoke to you the most from this book?

___
___
___
___
___
___
___
___
___
___
___
___
___
___

2) How will you incorporate the lessons from this book into your daily life?

3) What dream will you be working on, in order to accomplish God's purpose in your life right now? What is your timeline of completion?

_____

_____

_____

_____

_____

_____

_____

_____

_____

_____

_____

_____

_____

PRAYER

In the space below, write a prayer of appreciation. Thank God for keeping you even when the enemy wanted to kill you. In all things, give thanks.

_____

_____

_____

_____

_____

_____

_____

_____

_____

_____

_____

_____

_____

www.ingramcontent.com/pod-product-compliance
Lightning Source LLC
Chambersburg PA
CBHW071204160426
43196CB00011B/2194